Client Machine

Client Machine

The B2B System for Generating Clients

George Athan

Published by Spartagy Publishing.

Printed in the United States of America

ISBN 978-1-7323874-0-9

This publication is designed to provide accurate and authoritative information with regard to the subject matter covered. It is sold with the understanding that the publisher is not engaged in rendering legal, accounting, or other professional advice. If legal advice or other expert assistance is required, the services of a competent professional should be sought. The opinions expressed by the authors in this book are not endorsed by Spartagy Publishing® and are the sole responsibility of the author rendering the opinion.

Most Spartagy Publishing® titles are available at special quantity discounts for bulk purchases for sales promotions, premiums, fundraising, and educational use. Special versions or book excerpts can also be created to fit specific needs.

For more information, please contact:

Spartagy Publishing

www.spartagy.com

Toll Free: 1-800-300-0760

Or call +1(646) 397-0704

Table of Contents

Acknowledgements

I want to thank my family and friends, who have always shown an incredible amount of love and support throughout my journey. Although it's impossible to list everyone, I would like to dedicate this book to:

My mother, who has selflessly given so much of her own life to ensure I had all the tools to become the person I am proud to be today.

My father, who isn't here physically, but is always with me in spirit.

My brother Nick, for always pushing me past my limits and taking our conversations to the next level.

My sister Tina, who encouraged reading early in my childhood and introduced me to my passion for books.

Nono, Nona, Yiayia, Roberta, and Ed, for always being there for me without hesitation, especially when I needed it most.

Kevin Hogan, for urging me to write this book and mentoring me throughout the process.

And to Felissa, who has been the best friend and business partner anyone could ask for. Writing this book would not have been possible without you.

Truthfully, without all of you.

Foreword

by Kevin Hogan, International bestselling
author of *The Science of Influence and
The Psychology of Persuasion*

George Athan is a genius.

He won't tell you that, but I will.

That's the **first secret. *Let someone else tell your story for you.***

In the Facebook era we are familiar with narcissism and the personality defects it covers and exploits.

Almost every client I work with wants one thing:

Clients.

A smaller number come to me because they want happiness or love, but 85% ask me to help them build their business.

The Second Secret?

And what is a business?

A box of wood?
A box of bricks?
A landing page and products to go with it?
A marketing system?
A cutting-edge piece of technology?

Your business IS your potent relationship to a valuable client group.

If you see your 'business' as a building or money, or ANYTHING other than your clients you will end up back working for Bill's Garage in no time.

The Third Secret?

There's already someone out there doing what you say you're going to do.

...and there's a lot of 'em.

And as P.T. Barnum may have said, *"There's a sucker born every minute".*

Do this one thing for me: When you say 'it' do 'it' because you will stand out.

And standing out for doing 'it' seems tragic. And it is for society. But for you, you can win half the game by showing up because half of the rest of the group won't show up.

The Fourth Secret?

Money Matters

Come on, you say, of course it matters. In fact, one get rich guru suggests you chase money.

And that's funny because you will get a great deal of what you follow.

But it will be short lived, and you will be bankrupt or in deep trouble of another kind, before you know it.

Your psychiatrist, medical doctor, attorney and many others learned a profession that would, in part, bring them money.

And you'd be surprised how often it does not.

Don't chase money. Instead of running to the money someone left at the ATM machine, develop a rock-solid plan for you to be incredibly valuable to a group of people who then cannot afford to be without you.

Do people want to work with you or buy your products and services because of how much money you get from them?

I don't think so.

I think we hire people to help us get results.

In fact, that is absolutely true.

You hire someone because they will help you develop your business in some way. You hire a janitor. You hire a consultant. Both people are helping your business grow.

Please don't chase money. You're going to be ahead of the game if you think of your work as growing your clients in some critical way.

If you see dollar signs when you think of your client, get out of your business or learn to be valuable to them... and all of your future clients that are coming soon to a meeting with you.

The Fifth Secret?

You will discover that some clients are simply not worth having.

I look at my clients like my family. I love them. I get irritated with them.

I deeply care about them. I want their success. I live with them through their decisions.

I want you to invest a LOT of mental effort into every client you have.

If you don't who will?

Want your client to be with you for 5 years? 10 years? Then make sure it's obvious that your client is getting what they need.

Sadly there are clients that I've had that I simply didn't want to keep.

Recognize that not every relationship is worth having. In fact, I would argue that most are not. I would also argue that those that are worth keeping are like gold.

The Sixth Secret?

Have one kind of friend.

Someone once said, Kev you have a lot of business friends.

The idea had never crossed my mind.

I live in Minnesota where it's chilly in the winter. If you see someone on the side of the road in the winter and they are in desperate need of help, would you leave a 'business friend' to die in the cold?

Friends are friends.

Good friends are good friends.

I love that my friends are often 'business friends'. Treat people as if they matter to you (because ultimately, they MUST matter to you) and it will be hard for them to leave you.

The Seventh Secret?

Learn from those who have gone before you.

There are dozens of business models that are simply not going to be predictably profitable in the next two years. But there are a number that will be.

If you attempt to buck the odds, then realize that you will live or die by that decision.

That's why a mentor, consultant or coach could be (maybe) an excellent idea for you.

The mentor will see where the path falls off the cliff long before you will. They've already done it all. Pay attention and listen.

But...

Remember that not all mentors are created equally. In fact, I will go so far as to say that 80% of coaches, consultants and mentors aren't worth a rusty penny.

I apologize for my brutal honesty if you will heed the warning.

George Athan is an example of a man who gives you a 250-page resume.

The Client Machine gives you his philosophy, ideology, thinking process into the mind of someone who gets what a business really is.

George is a friend. I've known him for a decade and can tell you that he wants you to succeed.

He will be irritated with you if you don't and will show you how to get back on the track when you fall off.

In this remarkable tome you will find the necessary knowledge to gain clients and be valuable to them.

Apply the ideas. Note the tools. Consider the strategies. And then DO.

Client Machine is a Bible of Business Success.

And now... I'd like to introduce to you, a man who knows how you will get your new and best clients... Mr. George Athan of New York, NY.

Kevin Hogan,
International bestselling author of
The Science of Influence and
The Psychology of Persuasion

SECTION 1
FOUNDATION

Chapter 1

Introduction

By choosing to read this book, I already know a few things about you. You made the decision to pick up a nonfiction book on new client generation, while others chose to waste their time on distractions that would only provide them with short term gratification. This one decision will put you ahead of others, and it's this kind of decision that will propel your company or career to levels others will never reach. As a consultant, I can tell you that I've only come across two types of people in business; those that constantly learn so they can get an edge, and those that don't. I already know who's who by the type of project I get asked to be a part of. The fast-growing companies that want to get bigger, faster, and stronger just happen to be run by executives who constantly read and want an edge over their competition. The companies that are struggling and desperately need life pumped into them to survive are usually run by people that haven't had any new ideas in a while, and have been coasting in business (and life). I don't believe it's a coincidence. Those that are constantly growing and looking for an edge, eat the lunch of those who coast and hope for the best.

There's no judgement in my voice when I say this, I'm just stating facts. And for those of you who think that nothing's so black and white, that there are more categories in business than just growing or dying, there aren't. There are varying degrees of these two states, but make no mistake, if you are not growing in life or business you are dying. You're either moving up or being pulled down. There are no plateaus. Plateaus are a myth. If you're not burning fuel and fighting gravity to climb higher, that gravity is pulling you down and will do so until you crash. In business that gravity is called attrition.

When your business isn't bringing in new clients and it's living off your existing customer base, it is slowly dying. One by one your clients are getting picked off by competitors. Some customers move to a different area, so they're forced to find a new vendor. Others go out of business. Maybe someone in your customer service department pissed a customer off, so they decide to never do business with you again, just to prove a point. Or maybe, it's just that your client's nephew now sells similar services and they feel obligated to give the business to their family member. There are thousands of reasons customers leave and they all happen over time. Which means time is working for you, if you're generating new customers, or time is working against you, slowly killing your business.

Attrition isn't only killing your customer base. It's going after your products, your people, and everything associated with your business. Products that aren't constantly updated with more bells and whistles are getting crushed by products that are. The iPhone changed the mobile phone industry forever, and yet if you were to use the first version of the iPhone today, I'm sure you'd want to throw it in the garbage in frustration, because so much has evolved since that first iteration. How about your employees? They couldn't regress, could they? Your people are either getting sharper with continual training, or they're getting rusty because they haven't gone through training in a while. The reality is that we can't even say that a business, as a whole, is growing or dying because those who are at the top of their market know that they need to examine every individual component of the business and make sure that there is progress. Don't be fooled by activity or change. Anyone can keep themselves busy, and change is inevitable, but progress is forward movement.

When you're aiming for progress, the very first place to look is your client acquisition strategy. Without a constant flow of new clients, nothing else matters. The success or failure of your business starts with your ability to bring in new business. In helping organizations of all different shapes and sizes, in a wide array of industries, I can definitively tell you that one of the most common problems in sales is lack of structure. Specifically, most organizations lack a structured process that they can repeat over and over, to generate new clients again and again. And even large corporations that have carefully built a process can suffer because only some salespeople follow it, and only some of the time. This leaves large companies with the same disadvantage small and midsize companies have: not being able to generate new customers and clients on demand.

Many salespeople are just left to themselves to figure things out. Not only are business owners not supporting their salespeople, but what's worse, they are *relying* on salespeople to supply the formula for bringing in business. Since business owners and executives are struggling to figure out how to get more clients and bring in more accounts, they search for the answer by sifting through more and more resumes in the hopes that if they can just find a salesperson with enough experience, that person will come with the solution they need, or at least contacts that can be leveraged to generate new business. But what comes next when neither the salesperson nor management has a process that can consistently bring in new accounts? What happens when those contacts are exhausted? When no one has answers and the well has run dry, those salespeople are eventually let go, or they quit because they know it's eventually coming.

Turnover is extremely expensive, and what I just described is completely backwards. Just like all business processes, it's management's responsibility to ensure that the organization has a strong sales process in place and to ensure that all the salespeople are supported in their efforts. Salespeople should be given constant training on that process and supplied with all the tools they need to thrive. This way, the fate of the organization is not in the hands of the sales team. Management leads, the team follows. Now if you're a one-person organization, you can use this methodology to rapidly grow your business and then standardize the practices that you set, so that others can follow. If you are a salesperson reading this book, then use this methodology to become the top producer at your organization. When no one understands how you are getting the results you're getting, you may be asked to implement this for the entire team.

So, what is the big promise? This book will show you how to consistently generate new clients without having to cold call, tediously create content, or spend a dollar on advertising. I will show you how to develop a full client acquisition system that generates new clients on demand, whether you are doing this for yourself or for your organization with thousands of salespeople. *Client Machine* is written for those that want that advantage I described earlier. It's written for those of you who value working smarter over working harder and would rather save years of time and lost opportunity while trying to figure it out on your own.

What makes this book unique among sales books is the two perspectives it is written from. The first perspective comes from my experience as a business growth consultant, where my work is focused on creating structure and building processes to help companies move faster and grow more rapidly. Companies don't get far without standardized processes, because everyone moves in different directions. Without structure, scaling is impossible.

Since your goal isn't just to learn something new, but to take your business to the next level, this first perspective is vital to your achieving results. This holds true whether 'your business' means your sales numbers if you're a salesperson, or your total revenue if you're the CEO.

The second perspective comes from my fascination with, and years of research on topics like psychology, influence and persuasion, NLP, sales and marketing. I've had the privilege of working closely with experts like the master of persuasion himself, Dr. Kevin Hogan, author of 24 books and best known for his internationally bestselling classic, *The Psychology of Persuasion: How to Persuade Others to Your Way of Thinking.* For the last 22 years I've been obsessed with learning how we're wired and how we make decisions, in order to understand why we do what we do. I've taken the knowledge I've accumulated throughout my journey and designed a sales process that taps into how buying decisions are made. A process that can rapidly increase your sales pipeline, shorten your sales cycles, and generate all the clients you want. Big promise? Now it's time to deliver.

Chapter 2

Building the Foundation

This book is broken up into three sections; Foundation, Lead Generation Machine, and Sales Machine. *Client Machine* is a combination of two powerful individual processes that come together perfectly to systematically generate clients in line with what you can handle. It consists of building a lead generation machine that repeatedly fills your calendar with sales appointments, and a Sales Machine that converts those prospects to new clients. To effectively grow and scale your business, you must strategically build these two machines on a strong foundation. The first section is dedicated to showing you how to operate in a way that uses your resources wisely to get the highest return on your investments. These resources are your time, money, energy, team, technology and so on.

This book is aimed at salespeople, executives, and business owners alike. There's something, in fact many things, for everyone. Parts of this first section on foundation are written with the business owner and executive in mind, since they're the ones with the power to make structural changes in the organization. I also strongly urge salespeople to read this section and resist the temptation to jump right into lead generation and the sales process. There are plenty of valuable insights that you'd miss out by skipping ahead. You may also find yourself in a position to implement these strategies in your organization.

Creating a client machine without a sufficient foundation will severely limit your potential.

Customers Vs Clients

Before we begin, let's differentiate between the word customer and client. The word customer is defined as anyone who purchases goods or services from another. 'Customers' are often associated with transactional purchases; simple, short-term sales where the customer already knows what he or she needs, and where very little effort is required from the salesperson. On the other side of the spectrum, a client is defined as one that is under the protection or patronage of another; a dependent. 'Clients' are often associated with solution selling, which is a more complex process, involving the collaboration of both buyer and seller, in which the latter must first develop an understanding of the client's business, industry, and needs, in order to design a solution that solves problems and achieves their objectives. Since clients are more dependent on the person advising them, they tend to be much more loyal than customers. And since the value they receive is perceived to be much higher than the value a customer would get from a transactional sale, clients pay more money.

Regardless of what industry you're in, or how you currently describe your buyer, going forward you should consider them all to be clients. Simply adopting this label immediately defines your role and responsibilities, and instructs you to deliver in a way where you are valued more, and consequently paid more. That additional value comes from the added service of becoming their advisor. It's no longer about you selling a product or service; it's about you solving their problem. You're guiding them through their challenges, navigating through the rough waters to get them to safety. The experience you bring, the guidance you provide, and the comfort you supply during these challenging times is the value you bring and the premium you are paid. Imagine, a sales process so good that not only do you close more deals, but clients are happier, and you are paid a premium because of it? Since price correlates with value, this book will show you how to do just that.

Inbound Vs Outbound

Whenever I'm asked, "What should I do? What's better, inbound or outbound marketing?" I typically respond: "Would you rather have your left arm or your right arm?" After the initial confused look, the response to that is, "Well I'd rather have both to be honest". And that is the ultimate answer. But first let's understand where this division came from in the first place.

Marketing automation software companies like Hubspot were responsible for coining the term 'inbound marketing', and more importantly, they were also responsible for creating this inbound vs outbound environment in their clever marketing campaigns. Software like theirs was initially created to help businesses capitalize on incoming traffic and the leads generated from it. To help create a path for the prospect to go through, making the buying journey a positive experience and nurturing those leads until the prospect was ready to act. The truth is, this was desperately needed because most leads were being wasted by Sales and a CRM alone wasn't enough. Companies were spending a fortune generating those leads only to find out that their salespeople would call once and never follow up. One study showed that on average, salespeople were only calling leads 1.3 times, and most of those attempts ended with the salesperson never actually getting the prospect on the phone.

Marketing automation software combined with CRM's allowed companies to keep track of the leads, prioritize them, and create predetermined workflows for the sales teams to follow so that each lead was given exactly what was needed to help them move to the next stage of buying.

This was all well and good, except for one minor detail; this process assumed that your website had all this traffic in the first place. It worked for larger companies that had a brand name and were spending a ton of money on advertising. But it was completely useless to everyone else. What good is triggered email or creating a lead score if you're a small business with no incoming leads? It was pointless. As the technology got more sophisticated and marketing automation companies started popping up all over, they had to create a bigger pie instead of constantly dividing the existing one. To do this they had to create the need for their product, which they did by teaching small business owners how to drive traffic to their website. In turn, small business owners would then need marketing automation software, continuing the growth of this industry and developing a new norm for marketers. White papers were created, along with videos, infographics, and blog posts on how we should be creating content, so you could get the prospect to come to you as opposed to going after the prospect directly. They created this inbound vs outbound argument that said outbound is old school, tacky, and no longer worked. We were told that we would be bothering people if we approached them through outbound, that we'd be looked at as disruptive and disrespectful.

The timing of this propaganda couldn't have been more perfect. There was a major transition that was happening at the time. See, during the period right before that time, direct mail was a significant form of prospecting, but costs were increasing. As postage was increasing, long distance calling rates were rapidly decreasing until they eventually disappeared, thanks to unlimited calling packages through the internet. This created an environment where prospectors got most of their business by cold calling on the telephone. Just like everything else that gets saturated, prospects started getting more and more frustrated with these cold calls all day long, while salespeople were getting burnt out speaking to frustrated people all day, or worse, not getting through at all because gatekeepers were getting increasingly better at not letting any sales calls through. Right on cue, in comes the message that says outbound is evil, old school, and no longer works... BOOM... you have a whole new generation believing that it's better to have the prospect come to you.

Obviously, there are benefits having a prospect come to you, but there were many misleading factors in this argument, as well as other important considerations which were left out in making the case for inbound over outbound. So, let's go back to the choice of having one arm or another. I say I prefer both, just like inbound and outbound. But, if I were forced to pick one, that's easy - my strong arm! Now let me quickly explain why outbound is the strong arm.

People are drowning in content. With everyone saturating the market with their content, prospects can't possibly consume this much. With so much information being generated and the majority of it low quality because marketers think it's a race in quantity, your prospects aren't even reading your stuff.

Inbound marketing costs too much. Regardless of what they tell you in cost per lead, I will show you how to get the lowest cost, highest quality lead through outbound. Your competitors are writing articles, creating infographics, filming videos, and now even live streaming their messages, so you'd have to have a team of people constantly creating content just to stand out from all of the other content being published. Not only is this very costly, but in my opinion it's like screaming louder and louder in a room that is progressively getting noisier.

It takes too much time. Think about planting seed after seed, hoping that enough seeds are planted so that you can reap the rewards over time. An effective content strategy can take 12-18 months before it blossoms into consistent leads. If you think about live streaming, that's information that disappears after the livestream is over. Because the content game is so competitive, it's becoming more demanding. In order to compete, you now have to provide your information in real time, only for that information to be discarded after the livestream is over. At least a video is an asset that can be used repeatedly. With outbound you can get a lead, or even a new customer, tomorrow!

Inbound leads are terrible. Decision-makers don't research a list of vendors to choose from, nor are they the ones walking around tradeshows. High level decision-makers usually pass off these tasks to lower level employees, which means your sales team is spending all their time with people who can't make the YES decision, but who can easily make the NO decision by not including your company in their list of possibilities. You can't go above these people's heads because you risk creating an enemy instead of a champion, which means that you have to rely on them selling for you by passing your message on. The only issue there is that after you've given them a 45-minute demonstration of how your products or services will solve all their problems, this employee will, in turn, give a condensed, 3-minute summary to the decision-maker!

Let me briefly take you into the world of strategic outbound. You can identify which type of companies would feel the greatest positive impact from your products/services. You can create a list of companies that mirrors your biggest or best clients and go after them. You won't have to hope that the right type of company finds you. Let's think about all the hoping you would have to do. You would have to hope that:

- **The perfect company** (biggest profit potential or biggest impact) **would recognize that they have a specific problem you solve.**

- **After recognizing they have that problem, they would believe the type of solution you provide is the answer to that problem.** For example, if I think I don't have as much sales as I should have, there are many different solutions for this. I can look for sales trainers, want to hire more salespeople, look to purchase software, research 100 different marketing strategies, etc. But let's say the perfect company recognizes they need a solution like yours. You would have to hope that...

- **They stumble upon your content as opposed to someone else's.**

- **The content was so good it converted that prospect to a lead.**

- **And after all that... you're hoping that the person doing this happens to be the ultimate decision-maker.**

With strategic outbound you can:

- Generate a list of the most desirable target companies.
- Target the actual decision-makers.
- Do your research on them and their company before contacting them.

- Bring a problem to them in such a way that if they didn't previously realize it existed, now they will.
- Provide specific solutions based on industry experience and company research.
- Create awareness, interest, and desire so that they take action.

Don't let inbound marketers confuse you. Outbound marketing is not the same as mass marketing. The old-school methods of 'spray and pray' mass marketing are not welcome anywhere, but laser-targeted strategic outbound can bring you immediate sales tomorrow. I want to wrap up this topic by giving you a new view on outbound, a different perspective than the, "Outbound is too disruptive - You're bothering people" mentality that has been lingering in this politically correct new world. If I'd just found the cure to Cancer and knew my uncle, who I love, has been dealing with a lot going through it, you are damn right that I would disrupt whatever he was doing to let him know! I wouldn't care what he was in the middle of; I would feel obligated to immediately make him stop what he was doing and tell him the great news. He's in the middle of eating dinner with the family? Great, put me on speaker phone because everyone is going to love hearing the great news!

In no way am I suggesting that it's okay for you to wake your clients up at 5 a.m. or disrupt their dinner just because you're excited about your product, or that you think they should listen to your sales pitch. What I *am* saying is that if you truly have a fix for your prospect's biggest challenge and can provide information which will greatly impact their business, you have an *obligation* to bring it to their attention. For example, if I know that a prospect is struggling with getting new business and I know that they are hurting financially because they don't have an effective process in place, I'm not going to just sit there and let them die. When I have a simple solution that can mean millions of dollars in revenue for them, literally change their business, and provide a stable environment for their employees, I'm not going to stand by and hope that someone at that company stumbles across my content and reaches out to me. The right partnership means that it will benefit both parties, which means that it would be irresponsible for me not to approach them. It would be irresponsible to both of us.

I brought up the politically correct environment because it amazes me how so many people are so scared of causing offence they end up doing more damage by not helping. They're more concerned about ruining a relationship that doesn't even exist yet, just with the idea that someone might get offended by the approach. I can tell you that this mindset won't allow anyone to survive in business. If you start with a great product or service that you're so proud of that you feel the obligation to bring it right to the door of every man, woman, child on this earth so they can benefit from it, you will have a solid foundation. As a salesperson you have to fall in love with your product or service, or don't sell it. You won't be good at selling something that you think is anything short of amazing. If you're a business owner or executive, make sure that your team is innovating and working each day to make your product or service better. For those who provide a service that can't be innovated, then make sure your team gets better at delivering it, or differentiate yourself by catering to the client in a way that no one else does.

This book isn't about your products or services. It assumes you already have a great mousetrap. That's just the starting point. This book will show you how to take these great offerings and use them to systematically build new client relationships.

Chapter 3

Pitch the Niche

When we talk about a niche, this is one of those lessons that you already *know* but probably aren't following, or at least not to the extent you could. I love teaching things that someone already knows because we save time by not having to prove the concept. Implementation happens faster. I'll give you my perspective on niches anyway, just to build more leverage on following through, but my hope for you is that by the end of this topic you're excited about this principle and ready to take it to the next level in all your sales and marketing campaigns going forward.

When slow or no growth companies ask me for help, the first place I look is to see if they've chosen a niche to operate in or not. Companies that don't choose a niche to dominate never dominate anything and therefore struggle. This struggle comes from a fear that committing to one market may alienate other business that falls outside that market. In turn they try to be all things to all people, rarely becoming anything to anyone. Let me ask you who you would choose if you needed heart surgery? Would you go to your general practitioner or a heart surgeon? The choice is obvious. Now let's try something less dramatic. Imagine there's a dispute over your product name and now there's possible trademark infringement litigation. And, as luck would have it, you're also in the process of going through a divorce and need to hire an attorney. Would you use the same person for both? Probably not. Even if they assured you they were experienced in both areas, chances are you would look for both the best intellectual property attorney you could find (however you define best), and also the divorce attorney that best meets your needs. In fact, if someone told you that they had a lot of experience in both matters, you probably wouldn't think they were fully competent in either area.

Understanding Time, Speed, and Growth

The real power in picking a niche is how it affects the speed at which things happen. See, growth is important, but velocity determines the size of your company and the options you have for future decisions. Ultimately, velocity not only impacts but controls your destiny. Let me explain what I mean with a visual. Let's suppose your company falls into one of the buckets below. For demonstration purposes, let's say that your company generates just under $5M in annual sales, which means that it will be found in bucket A.

If your company does that same $5M in sales, except this time you get that done in only 6 months instead of 12, now your company is on track to do $10M a year in sales and you'd be in bucket B. Taking that example further, if you can hit those $5M in sales in only 3 months' time and do this every quarter, you've now moved to bucket C. Like I said, the significance of these revenues goes far beyond my buckets in this demonstration. A company in bucket C is taken far more seriously than bucket A and has many more resources to create more product lines, enter new markets, acquire companies, and therefore multiply faster.

Now that we understand the importance of speed, let's dig a little deeper to discover the two main areas of speed you need to focus on to achieve rapid growth.

1. **The speed of making a sale.** This involves any and every sale, from acquiring a new customer to upselling and cross selling. The faster you can convert clients and generate new sales, the faster you can start working on the next one. Think about all the time it takes to follow up and get the person on the telephone or try to coordinate an in-person meeting. Meetings can be pushed back days, and often weeks at a time. If you add up that time, accounting for all the prospects and existing clients you deal with throughout the year, what would that wasted time amount to? More importantly, how much more business would you have if you used that wasted time to generate more clients? If you have a sales team, that number just multiplied.

2. **The speed of delivering the goods or services.** This is your back end. Your company has a certain capacity and it's important that your front-end sales machine isn't bringing in more business than you can deliver from the back end. As much as it seems like it's a good problem to have, it isn't. This is where customers become dissatisfied and leave you. Not only do they never come back, and you forever lose their business, but it creates a long ripple effect of lost revenue. Dissatisfied customers hurt your reputation on their way out, robbing you of additional future revenue.

When you're not able to properly deliver on your offering, whether that means physically delivering a product, or performing to the level you promised, you create a ton of work for yourself (or others) in dealing with an unhappy customer. And every minute you spend communicating with a customer about a prior purchase you're no longer getting paid from, decreases the profitability of that transaction. Conversations of this nature require time and energy from you or your team, and when you burn these resources on completed transactions, it removes focus from delivering to new paying customers, affecting both your output and revenue. Your goal is to be able to deliver your value to that customer in an exceptional way through to completion, so you can move on to the next one. If you do this effectively, the only need for additional conversations would be because the customer is considering additional purchases.

These two items should be focal points for your entire operation. Regardless of what you sell, think of your business as a manufacturing company which must produce and deliver, over and over again. On the front end you're manufacturing clients and producing sales. The initial raw materials to manufacture clients are a list of names of prospects, scheduled on your calendar, and the information that you have to help them. Through your manufacturing process, this list of names goes into your client machine on one end and on the other side a new client is created, and a transaction is produced. Your goal is to follow this process repeatedly, producing as many clients in the shortest period of time as possible. The second thing you manufacture is whatever it is that you are delivering to that client. Your team takes this new order and delivers the value you promised, in a fast and exceptional way. Neither speed nor quality can be compromised.

You'll continue this cycle of selling and delivering, again and again, to both new and existing clients. Your existing clients will feel more comfortable making larger purchases more frequently as you complete each cycle. With your client machine generating new clients on the front end, you can offer even more value through additional products or services, generating more revenue throughout the lifetime of the relationship. The faster you can effectively sell and the more cycles you can complete in a shorter period of time, the higher the lifetime value of each new client becomes. The increase in the number of clients, multiplied by the increase in lifetime value of each client, becomes exponential business growth.

Speed Growth by Niche

Let's get back to what this has to do with a choosing a niche, and how doing so will accelerate your growth. Many of you reading this book are business owners or executives of companies with teams of people. To demonstrate the point, let's consider the solopreneur, a one-person operation, where time is the biggest challenge. After proving the point as a solopreneur, it will be easy to see the impact when you multiply this to reflect a team. Suppose you're a marketing consultant hired by a dentist to create a marketing campaign for his practice. The dentist asks you to create the step-by-step process his team should follow to bring in new business. You are to create all the copy for direct mail campaigns, email, and scripts his team should use. You and the dentist agree on a fee of $15,000 for all the work you will do.

To do this effectively, you start with your discovery process, to ensure a complete understanding of his practice, including the ideal customers to target, the procedures that will be offered, pricing, and the differentiating factors that brought the existing customers to this practice. After your discovery, you research other campaigns that dentists have used to get extraordinary results, so you can model some of those campaigns or at least pull some ideas out of them. That initial $15,000 project sounded lucrative, but you quickly start to realize the more work that goes into this, the more the value diminishes. Now it's time for you to create. You write and rewrite all the different pieces that will go into this campaign. Finally, when you think most the work is over, you still have to test. You do small mailings to test different variations of the marketing pieces to see what people are responding to, so you get the highest response rates from all your efforts. When all is said and done, you've spent two months on this project and now that it's over, it's time to find more clients.

Let's start with the capacity perspective, number 2 on our previous list: **The speed of delivering the goods or services.**

In the scenario above, if you're a marketing consultant without a niche then you will only be able to handle a few clients at one time. Imagine having to do a different discovery, research, writing, testing, and finalizing for every new client you have, because they come from a number of different industries. At most you'd be able to handle a few per month (effectively), limiting your income to $150-$300k a year. Keep in mind, we haven't even discussed the fact that it would take time to speak to prospects and sell before you even get the projects. Now, let's reimagine you as that marketing consultant, but focused on working exclusively with dentists. Now you have this great process which you just spent two months perfecting. It's all mapped out and you have amazing copy written for direct mail pieces, email, and even telephone or in-person scripts practices can use. Why not sell this entire system to another practice that doesn't compete with your client? What if you sold it to one dentist in every state? That's 50 clients for the work you just did for one. In fact, you can easily find two dentists per state that can't possibly serve the same demographic, because people will only travel so far from their home. The point is, from a capacity perspective, you can easily handle 100 of these clients this year. By choosing a niche, you can deliver your services better and faster, allowing you to increase your revenue to $1.5M a year (100 x $15,000).

Now let's try another scenario. Imagine your business provides detergents and soaps to chain restaurants in New York City. Your competitor sells detergents and soaps, but they sell it to anyone, anywhere. They don't want to 'limit' themselves. This means they have accounts spread out in different locations and they sell to different types of establishments like restaurants, hotels, and catering halls. Who do you think will sell a million dollars' worth of soap faster? From a capacity perspective, you will. For those of you not so familiar with the scene, getting in and out of New York City is time consuming and costly. Because your accounts are all consolidated in one area, you are centrally located and can deliver to all your accounts in one day while your competitor has drivers going through all five boroughs and beyond. Because you deal with just restaurant chains, your customers do volume with you, and they go through product faster with all their locations. Also, because you deal with restaurant *chains*, logistically delivering your product is so much easier because it's the same process for all the franchised restaurants.

Let's move on to the other very important speed benefit of choosing a niche: **The speed of making a sale.**

Going back to our marketing consultant example, would you expect it to be easier or harder to sell your services to another dentist, compared to let's say, an attorney? Obviously, the dentist is easier. You already have proof of concept, a testimonial, and a reference your new prospective dentist can speak to. Can you use that same testimonial or reference for the attorney? Sure. It just won't hold the same weight because the process you created for the dentist won't necessarily work for the attorney, who's also hoping you'll do the same great job for their industry. So how about you focus on selling this just to dentists, and now you have 10 different dentists who will speak highly of your services? Will that make things even easier when approaching the next dentist? Of course! Soon you become unstoppable. Plus, the moment you tell your prospects that you only serve the dental industry, you completely eliminate competition. No longer are you competing with every marketing consultant in the world. Now, you're only competing with marketing consultants who specialize in serving dental practices. And the great news for you is that most of your competitors are as scared of picking a niche as you once were. So, the truth is, once you do this you won't have any competition.

Dominating One Market at a Time

To create rapid growth, everyone in your business must be proactive. This is the exact opposite of what typically happens for slow growth companies. Slow growth executives constantly find themselves in a reactive state, and these reactions are what actually slow growth down. Think of the saying 'one step forward, two steps back.' Those two steps back were the result of some negative event which happened in the business, and what we call reactions are the effort we make to fix it or control the damage. But when we're constantly reacting, we're exerting as much energy as if we're moving forward, just without the progress, because all we're doing is compensating for the steps we've taken backwards. If you do this often enough, you'll feel like a hamster on a wheel.

So, to avoid that scenario, the proactive approach you need to take is to choose a niche and go down the line, piercing through that market. The top 1% in all categories go deep, rookies go wide. The big fear everyone has is that they'll miss opportunities that fall outside their market. You may still ask, "What if this additional business outside my niche finds me, while I'm hunting for the business that falls in my niche?" I'll double down and caution you that anything outside your expertise requires you to learn, which requires more of your time and that time is expensive. Getting involved in markets that are outside your wheelhouse will require you to move much slower and this extra time will cost you more revenue in comparison to sticking to your niche. Obviously, in some cases it may be irresponsible for you to turn away business, so in those cases do what you must. But throughout the process, think about what it will cost you in time to actually get the business and deliver the best possible product/service flawlessly. Anything less than the best will cost you.

The good news is that once you've dominated your market there are many different markets to expand into. You can go one-by-one, dominating each space until you've officially conquered the world. But until you've dominated one market, it wouldn't make sense to waste the effort just being a drop in another bucket. There's no benefit to spreading yourself thin. We can see how each effort can compound your business if you build upon and use all of your previous efforts. Each case study, testimonial, reference, or industry award can be used to further dominate more of that specific market. Social proof mounts until you are recognized by everyone as the leader in that market. In a world full of generalists, you'll be a specialist. And just like outdated methods of mass marketing, your competitors will still be using the antiquated approach of mass appeal, yet never appealing to anyone.

Think About One Buyer (at a Time)

In sales, you often hear phrases like, "It's a numbers game" or "On to the next one." At first, they seem innocent enough. They just sound like a positive way to stay persistent so that you don't become discouraged and give up. But be warned. These sayings originated from a mindset that would be harmful to your business or sales career if you adopted that mentality in today's business environment. This mindset attempts to compensate for something that is ineffectual, by increasing volume. This delusional and destructive mindset says it's okay to reach out to people that aren't the right fit, just as long as you reach out to enough people to get the job done. That might work for the sales manager who's stuck in 1984, but that doesn't work for all the people whose time is completely wasted, getting absolutely no value out of the exchange. The damage isn't limited to the names on that bad prospect list. Even more damage is being done to the salespeople facing constant rejection by a large number of unqualified people, who would never be able to give a positive response in the first place. I see this mentality every day when we get a terrible cold email written by someone who's not taken the time to learn what people respond to. Or even worse, I get an email pertaining to something that has nothing to do with us, never mind being able to add value. When these people don't get any positive responses from sending their garbage out, the only solution they come up with is, "I must need to send to a larger list".

Yes, more of something *can* compensate, but you want to maximize first and then multiply so that you're compounding the positive effects to get exponential results. Mass marketing, blanketing crowds, is just as ineffective as not having a niche. Again, it's trying to appeal to everyone and never appealing to anyone. The top 1% of marketers has moved to a laser-targeted sniper approach to marketing. What would happen to your response rates if you reached out to specific people with a message that is so personal, offering a solution that seems so customized to the individual problem that person is experiencing, and using words that seem like they were only meant for them in their unique situation? Your results would go through the roof because those messages are hard to ignore. But the numbers game mentality builds a gigantic list consisting of many different market segments. In order for your copy to speak to all those different segments at once, your language has to be very generic. That general language may allow you to talk to a large number of people at once, but specifics and personalization is what actually creates interest and gets a response. So what good is speaking to everyone at once if what you're saying isn't getting anyone's interest?

At the same time, we must balance being effective with being efficient. Although a manually written ultra-personalized message may be the most effective, it would severely limit us because we only have so much time in a day. Imagine if you didn't have to compile a list at all. Wouldn't it be great if you had some amazing piece of software that was able to analyze millions of conversations on social media, read blog posts along with the comments below, and sift through online reviews to find your next perfect prospect? Can you imagine if you had some way of knowing who the one person is that needs your product or service more than anyone else in the world? If you were able to pinpoint with that accuracy, your sales process would be quick and easy. With that kind of precision targeting, you wouldn't need to reach out to even one other person since you can only have one conversation at a time. And when you're done helping that person then you would move to the next highest value target.

Maybe Artificial Intelligence will get us there someday, but the point is if we could target that well, we would target the best prospects and just pick them off one at a time instead of mass marketing. The closest thing to that technology today is to focus on that one perfect buyer and then create a profile of that person, known as a Client Avatar or Buyer Persona. It allows you to personify your target market and speak to them in a way that will resonate with your best buyers. You can segment your lists and create a persona for each segment. You can speak to a thousand people that fall under that one persona and yet everyone would feel like you are speaking only to them. Who are the people in your niche that you are targeting? What do you know about them? What do they like and dislike? The deeper you go in targeting, the more personalized you can make your message, directly tapping into their fears, frustrations, ambitions, and desires.

When building your personas, start with the business, and then move to the economic buyer. Consider the following factors:

- **Sector**
- **Industry**
- **Company Size (# of Employees, Revenue, Market share)**
- **Company Age or Stage in Lifecycle**
- **Executive Title**
- **Gender**
- **Age Range**
- **Years at Company**
- **Responsibilities**
- **Goals/Objectives**
- **Challenges**
- **Interests/Passions**
- **Likes/Dislikes**

One last thing on this topic: sometimes I see people try to create personas that are too specific and not realistic of the entire group. They create these back stories based on a couple of real life examples. Just because two people like surfing, obviously, that doesn't mean to speak to all your prospects about the beach. But you *will* find some commonalities among your entire group. For example, the software industry is very sophisticated with regard to sales. I find that most executives in the tech world continually educate themselves in the latest sales best practices. Furthermore, some executives spend more time learning sales strategies than others, just because of their day-to-day responsibilities. So, if you were to approach a sales-savvy executive such as the VP of Sales, who operates in a sales-savvy industry like SaaS, and you were to contact them using an old-school sales approach, you would expect to get a very negative response. In other words, don't expect to get anywhere using telemarketing and not taking the time to do a little research on the company. By not following certain etiquette, you will consistently fail with this buying persona. Yet, you may use the same method to approach an executive in the manufacturing industry and you'll have better luck. Build your Buyer Personas and look for these types of observations. Your campaigns will be much more successful because of your ultra-personalized approach and messaging.

> **Resource:** Download the Ideal Client Profile sheet that I personally use to create Client Avatars. You can download your copy at www.client-machine.com/ICP

Focus on Your Next 100 Prospects

You're building your target list and you're ready to take over the world. Using the 'Dentist' example earlier, when doing your research, you find that you can purchase a list of 154,000 dental practices across the country. In your excitement you make your purchase and you're off to the races. Great, now what? Can you afford to do a 150k+ direct mail campaign? Maybe, but even if so it wouldn't be cost effective to do one large campaign like that. Can you make 154,000 calls? No, not unless you do robocalls, and you're smart enough to know that's not the answer. Can you email that many? Yes, but again now you're back to speaking very generally when personalization is the key to getting high responses. The trick is to break down the list into small segments and the smaller the segment the more you can personalize. The goal is to focus on the first 100 prospects, speaking to one very specific persona and personalize it as much as you can. Then you can worry about the other 153,900. The number 100 isn't a fixed rule. The rule is breaking your list up into as many small pieces as possible and to personalize the message as far as you can. Do this repeatedly.

I want to give you an example outside of our B2B world to demonstrate how important segmentation and personalization is for everyone. This especially comes into play when you're writing your outreach campaigns later. Years ago, a friend of mine had a martial arts studio and was looking to grow the business. As a friend, and as a student that wanted the school to grow, I created multiple marketing campaigns and a sales process so that we would have a steady flow of new students enrolling. The student base started growing pretty rapidly, and within just a couple of months we needed a much larger training facility. My buddy Chief, (short for Chief Instructor), found a facility four times the size of his original studio. The size of the new facility would allow him to continue to grow the business, but it also meant moving his school into a new city. Although there was risk in losing existing students, the move created an opportunity to market to an entire new geography and capture more customers. This new location also gave him the opportunity to offer fitness training on the days there were no martial arts classes. Those that weren't interested in martial arts, now had another reason to become a customer.

We moved to the new location and created a campaign that went door to door bringing awareness to all the local neighbors about crimes that had happened within a 10-mile radius over the past 6 months. They were surprised to hear the number of robberies and violent crimes that were happening not too far from their homes. The campaign goal was to bring awareness and provide solutions to protect themselves and their families. As a thank you to the new neighborhood that was welcoming us, we offered several free self-defense classes where anyone who lived in the neighborhood could learn the basics of self-defense. We provided residents with a list of emergency contact telephone numbers, and specific instructions on how to handle almost any emergency situation from home invasions to smelling smoke. Not only were the residents happy about the new self-defense gym moving into the neighborhood, but they were also happy to answer our survey questions about what was most important to them. We asked questions like, "What appeals to you more about our new facility, self-defense training or physical fitness?" and, "Why is that important to you?"

Although going door to door speaking to people was a very time-consuming task, the data that we got from it was incredible. We knew the names, addresses, contact information, and specific preferences of hundreds of residents. For those that had no interest in self-defense but had an interest in physical fitness, they were only sent marketing on fitness and health. For the men who responded that their biggest concern was not being able to protect the women in their lives when they weren't home, they were sent marketing pieces on special training classes designed for men and women to train together. Many of these new students initially came in because of self-defense but found a new hobby that they could do together to bring them closer in their relationships. The point is that everyone has different preferences, and what appeals to some cannot possibly appeal to all. By appealing to each segment's preferences, this martial arts academy outgrew their new location in less than one year!

Could this same result have been achieved by blanketing the entire neighborhood with mailings? Sure. But that falls back on the destructive and delusional mindset that we mentioned earlier. To reference this behavior when we see it, let's call it the *Numbers-Game Mentality*. It represents the old school mentality of marketing and sales, where you increase the volume of your efforts in order to compensate for inefficient or ineffective practices. You may ask, "What would make it ineffective if the same result is achieved?" Let's start with my 92-year-old grandmother we call Yiayia.

Although she doesn't live in the neighborhood of the martial arts school, she represents many other elderly men and women who do live there. No matter how much crime is happening in her neighborhood, Yiayia will never be taking a self-defense class. Again, no matter how amazing your technique to shed fat or what state-of-the-art equipment you've developed to build strength, you are not getting this cute old lady into your gym. New price promotions? It can be free and she's still not going.

This means that you could send her a mailing every day for the rest of her life and you will never get her as a customer. Knowing that, would it still be worth continuing or should you just never mail her again? On the other hand, there are people in that same neighborhood that are prime prospects and just had not said YES *yet*. Maybe they're in a contract with their gym waiting for it to expire in a few months before they join yours. Maybe they're interested in martial arts but have a big project at work that will keep them busy, so the next two months are not good for them. They'll reconsider in the summer time. Would it make sense to never mail these prospects again just because right now is not a good for time for them to join?

Herein lies the problem with the approach followed in most people's marketing efforts. They waste resources like time, money, and energy, contacting people that will never be a good fit and will never buy, and they give up too early on the prospects that are a fit but just haven't responded yet. By segmenting your lists into tiny categories, you can stop wasting time and money on what can never work, so you have more resources to allocate to what can. The results you get will amaze you. It's said that on average people need to come in contact with a brand at least 7-9 times before making a purchase. Can you see how easy it is to blow a budget on a big list and run out of gas before you contacted all the good prospects the appropriate number of times needed to get a response? Just remember, amateurs go wide, pros go deep. One last mention, I use the word *mailing* in this example because of the nature of the business we described and the fact that the most obvious cost in mailings is financial. The word mailings can easily be substituted with *calls, emails*, or *LinkedIn messages*. Since most of these outreach efforts won't impact your budget at all, the resource that will be depleted most is time, which is much more expensive than money. I intentionally used an example that has a hard cost because in my experience, people don't value their time nearly as much as they value money, when realistically it's the same thing.

Chapter 4

Differentiating

If someone hasn't chosen a niche, they really haven't defined what market place they're in. And because they never wanted to be confined to one market, they were never really able to articulate what it was that makes them the best choice for customers in that market. This is known as differentiating. As a self-preservation mechanism, our brain has an instinctive need to define the world around us, and we do this by creating associations and labels for things. When a stranger walks up to your door, your brain has to determine what that means before you can create a plan of action. If you identify this person as a threat, you may decide to call 911 or grab a shotgun. If you recognize the name of his company on his uniform and he shows you his lanyard with his identification, you may label him a salesperson and put the shotgun down.

For some, the shotgun is the proper response when seeing a salesperson, but hopefully that's not the case for you with your sales background or entrepreneurial spirit! The part of our brain that's 2 million or so years old and known as the reptilian brain, has this insatiable need to understand what things are by putting a label on them. It will stop every conscious thought until it has defined the world around it with that label. Our advantage is in knowing that this label doesn't have to be created by the observer but can in fact be created by the marketer. We've seen the dairy industry use this to their advantage with their *Milk Does a Body Good* campaigns in the 1980's. Milk has been proven to be harmful to the human body, but that slogan, repeated often enough, had the masses believing otherwise. The 'Milk Mustache' campaigns came later to reinforce the drink's nutritional value with young mothers and twenty-something buyers.

For years industries have spent billions of dollars trying to create neuro-associations in our minds, linking their products to benefits that often do not exist. People drinking store-bought orange juice for its health benefits and the healthy associations with Vitamin C, only to realize later that it's just as much of a sugary drink as soda. On the opposite end of the spectrum, there are many small to midsize companies with products that have amazing benefits, and yet the market has no idea of their immense value because the company has done a poor job of communicating it, aka, differentiating. To understand the value of one thing, often we must compare it to something else. Our perception is our reality and that reality is relative. Is 70 degrees considered warm? It depends. If it's in December and you expect 20-degree weather, then yes, it's warm. But if we're in August, that 70 degrees may feel chilly. Why does this matter to your business? It matters because in order for your potential customers to be able to make a decision in choosing your product versus another, they have to put a label or value on it first. Remember the example of not knowing to call 911 or to answer the door until you were able to put a label on the person walking to your door? The label influences the course of action taken. Your prospect can't decide if they should choose your product or your competitors until they have more information to compare the two.

Relationship – Differentiation – Price

Your prospects are going to decide who they buy from using one of three methods: Relationships, Differentiation, or Price. Let's go through them to give you the best chances of the decisions going in your favor. Starting with relationships, a prospect may decide to buy from you based on a relationship he or she has with someone at your organization. This is where you get your repeat buyers. With each purchase, it becomes easier and more reasonable to make the next purchase from the same organization. Typically, people are creatures of habit and the smallest act of kindness can create a bond that brings a customer back repeatedly. These relationships are your 1st degree connections. Your prospect can also choose your company based on a relationship they have with someone else, who in turn has had some type of relationship with your organization. These 2nd degree connections are what you call referrals. Referrals are highly effective because bonds are created relatively fast. All the necessary goodwill, positive experiences, and admiration transfer from the previous relationship. Finally, your 3rd degree connections are recommendations people take from complete strangers like review sites or connections on social media they don't know personally. The experiences and reviews of others very easily persuade people, even if they are written anonymously online. It is important to understand how all these relationships are influencing your buyer's behavior, because they often look to do business with those they've already done business with, or with those who others have tried, before choosing to be the guinea pig themselves. This is the reason social proof has such an impact on our decisions.

So this tells us how we should operate going forward. Our goal is to build a client machine that's constantly generating new relationships. The more client relationships you have, the more your business can grow exponentially on the back end. The lifetime value of a new client is worth substantially more than that first transaction. It will be easier for your clients to purchase additional products or services from you then to find someone else with a similar offering. Knowing this, we want to systematically generate new relationships, and maximize those relationships by continuously recommending additional purchases.

Price and Differentiation

We'll discuss price and differentiation together because they go hand and hand. Very simply, if a prospect has no idea what makes two vendors different then the only way they know how to decide is based on price. Since the two options are exactly the same, they'll always go with the lower priced option because that provides the most benefit. This is a dangerous game to play because very rarely do companies do well in business by being the lowest priced. In fact, except for Walmart, I don't know any business that survives this deadly game. Usually, it would benefit you more to increase prices because the amount of the increase goes straight to your bottom line and most of the time this increase doesn't affect sales (depending on the size of the increase). Choosing to lower prices as a differentiator is a race to the bottom because each reduction comes right off your bottom line. For those that think discounting creates a good incentive to drive sales, the math just does not work out. The increase in sales is rarely ever enough to compensate for the volume that would be required to bring in the same amount of profit.

How to Differentiate Effectively

It's important to understand all the competitors in your space and know everything about them. Their company, product, pricing, and what exactly they are delivering to the end user. Salespeople who don't know about their competitors are being lazy and leaving too much to chance. This lack of research and appropriate messaging forces the customer to figure out the differentiating factors on their own and make the purchase themselves, as opposed to the salesperson clearly educating prospects as to why their offering is different and what makes that difference better, and ultimately making the sale. The customer buying and the salesperson selling may seem the same, but as far as getting a deal closed, the first approach relies on hope while the other relies on performance. If you don't know what your competitors are offering, you take the risk of never differentiating in the market and throwing away sales that should have rightfully been yours. How can you say you're different if you have no idea what your competitors are offering? And how can you tell prospects that you're better if you don't know what makes you different?

By choosing a niche, you have committed to dominating a submarket. This means that you are absolutely the perfect choice for some and a terrible choice for others. Your goal is to attract the clients you are perfect for and repel those that are not a great fit. Differentiating clearly draws lines in the sand. Although you will be pushing some away, you quickly make up that loss, and then some, by making it an easier decision for your ideal prospects. These are the prospects that become raving fan clients. And since our goal is to systematically target and convert these prospects, we're then going to need a message that speaks to them directly and resonates so well that it's like magic to their ears. In the section labeled Sales Machine, you'll learn an incredible process for creating those messages.

For now, start to think about who gets the biggest benefit from buying your product or service? Get as specific as possible. Who do you have the most impact on? Your raving fans are going to be those that get the most value from your offering. Who are they?

Exercise:

When differentiating, you're only asking two questions: "What makes us different?" and "Why is that better?" Do you have a secret sauce or a better approach? Is your team qualified or better credentialed? Are your clients exclusive or do you have more clients than your competitors? Differentiating allows you to own your market because the only people who can even provide the same level product or service would have to have that differentiating factor- which they don't. This means you have no competition: effectively a monopoly.

Reach out to your 10 of your best clients and ask for a few minutes of their time in return for a small reward. Explain that they are your ideal clients and you are looking to find clients that are as wonderful as they are. Ask them to tell you in their own words, what it is that makes your company or product different. When you understand the differentiating factor, it's important to understand why that mattered to them when choosing you. Here's the gem in this exercise, it doesn't matter what you think makes you better, it matters what your customers think. Furthermore, it matters what your best customers think because that is what you want more of. Look out for certain words or phrases that are repeated by multiple clients in this exercise. These phrases will most likely resonate very well with other buyers within this persona and they'll be drawn to your message as you are speaking their language.

How to Create Killer Case Studies

It's important to align the right offering with your best buyer, using the most effective messaging. Start with your ideal buyers in mind, then figure out which product or service would be best to get your foot in the door. Once that's complete, create the marketing that's going to bring those two together. In the exercise above, you'll have the opportunity to get a ton of great feedback from the people who matter most, your best clients. During this interview, you should ask questions that will lead to the ultimate case study. Before determining what those questions are, let's quickly review what makes a killer case study.

Case studies are often very digital, filled with numbers, and boring to read, which is the exact opposite of what you want. We've all heard how left-brain thinking uses more logic, while the right brain is more creative and emotional. What's fascinating is that these two seem to share resources, meaning that the more you crunch numbers and analyze, the less emotional you are in that moment. This is why someone could come off as cold at times if they're focused too much on facts. It's also true that if you ever find yourself extremely emotional, there is almost no logic to your thinking in that moment. This is vital to know because when it comes to making purchases, we buy with emotion and justify later with logic. The very action of making a purchase is purely emotional and if we want our case studies to influence our buyers to take action, then we must make them as emotional as possible. To do this, we must tell a story. Stories force the listener or reader to put themselves in the shoes of the main character. The reason a good movie has the power to make us happy or sad, or produce all kinds of other emotions is because we identify, that is to say, we imagine what it would feel like to go through all the experiences the character or characters in the movie go through. The same identification should be happening with your case studies.

During your interview with your best buyers, ask what exactly it was that they were feeling before hiring your company or buying your product. Ask about their environment, the fears, the frustrations. What was it exactly that they were worried about? What would it mean for them if they never found a solution? When building your case study, it's important that you create the narrative of before, during, and after coming in contact with your product or company. Take them through the stories of the other options they had before choosing you. This is going to mirror your new prospect's current environment.

Let your case study tell the story of why your customer thought you were different, why those differences mattered to them in making the decision, and then what the outcome was. Telling a boring story of how you increased production 34% does nothing for anyone. Bring them through an emotional journey that they can relate to. They can relate because these are prospects that have the same buyer persona as your case study. Ask your current clients how they felt when you showed the results you did and why that was important for them. Ask them to talk about future opportunities that have developed because of the great decision they made choosing you, your product, and/or company.

This is how you create a killer case study. I recommend you use the above exercise not only to help you differentiate yourself in the market, but also to construct your sales pitch by building on those previous customer experiences and sharing them with your new prospects.

SECTION 2

LEAD GENERATION MACHINE

Chapter 5

Multiplying Your Business by Multiplying Your Leads

A fast growth company can only grow as quickly as the sales opportunities come in, and it always starts with generating leads. Obviously, you can repeatedly sell to your existing customer base but there's only so much they can buy. For rapid growth, you constantly need new clients, and to get clients you consistently need to generate sales meetings with prospects to have the opportunity to convert them. I purposely say sales meetings because people use the word 'leads' to describe many different things. Just so there's no confusion with terms like suspects, prospects, lists, lead, marketing qualified lead, sales qualified lead, or opportunity, let's be clear. **We want a consistent flow of qualified prospects who meet (via telephone or in person) with a salesperson to engage in a sales conversation about their business challenges or goals so you can offer your product or service as a solution.**

Without a constant flow of these sales meetings, you won't have a fast growth company. New client acquisition must be constant, new strategic partnerships should be forged, and an ongoing effort to continue this expansion should happen from every angle. Every minute of every business day should be a minute that's being used to create awareness, build new relationships, and deepen your market penetration. If not, there's another salesperson on another sales team at your competitor's company, who's calling your potential next client right now. One of the reasons why many small businesses without a sales team struggle is because the business owner, wearing many hats, is responsible for sales. This means every moment that they're working on bookkeeping or servicing an existing client, that company stopped growing. Fast growth companies don't have an off switch for sales. There's no pause, it's just always on. Companies with sales teams, who don't have a constant flow of sales opportunities, have the same dilemma. The moment the flow of sales meetings stops, the company stops growing.

A friend of mine was recently diagnosed with sleep apnea. The way he describes it is that throughout the night he often finds himself without air. Just for a moment, his body forces itself to wake up (gasping) so that he can again take in the oxygen he needs. This is a survival mechanism because the nervous system understands that it needs oxygen to live and makes that the main priority. He then falls back asleep, loses oxygen, wakes up, and this cycle continues to happen repeatedly throughout the night. Even though he may sleep for seven to eight hours, he says he never feels rested. He never gets the chance to get into a deep state of sleep because he is constantly running out of that flow of oxygen, putting his sleep on hold. The long-term effects of sleep apnea could lead to heart failure, stroke, cancer, and ultimately death. This is a perfect metaphor for business. Sales opportunities (leads) are like oxygen for the business. We need a steady flow of them where we never run out because when we run out, even for a moment, our growth is on hold.

Imagine a salesperson with back-to-back sales meetings in their calendar. They're a top producer, generating a very high rate of return on investment for the company. In contrast, imagine the typical salesperson that spends 20% of their day engaging in sales activity. Of their eight-hour day, less than two hours are spent discovering a prospect's needs, presenting, closing, and overcoming objections. Why are you paying them the other 6 hours? Without a steady flow of opportunities for your sales team to sell, your business is dying. It's not dying like the obvious choking to death, it's much subtler than that. It's more like gasping for air, one wasted hour at a time, until your survival mechanism steps in to sell just enough to continue to survive, and ultimately leading to the long-term heart failure or Cancer of the business. Think about companies with large sales teams that have gaps in their calendar because they don't have enough leads. The bigger the team, the more gaps of time without selling, the more damage being done to the company.

To Pitch or Not to Pitch, Consultative Sales is Out of the Question

Just like inbound marketing, there's a time and place for consultative selling, but the initial stage of an outbound marketing campaign is not it. Your goal is to create processes that will allow you to be proactive in your approach to building your business rapidly. To do that using outbound, we must bring our 'foot-in-the-door' product (or service) directly to the people who need it most, who have the budget, and the authority to say YES. To create an outbound campaign that's going to generate meetings with decision makers we must sell the meeting, which means this is more of a pitch. The consultative sales approach is very effective when you're going through your discovery process or doing a needs analysis, because it demonstrates that your goal is only to find the best solution for the client, not to force one specific solution down their throat. Consultative selling works well in inbound marketing because the prospect is coming to you and, like a doctor, you must understand everything that's going on before you can make a diagnosis. But when you're the one approaching and asking for a busy executive's time, you must immediately offer something of value in exchange for that time. The best way to do this is to go in with knowledge of the challenges your prospect is facing and offer to provide a solution to those problems. Your research will give you the knowledge you need, and list segmentation ensures that you are speaking directly to the needs of each prospect. Also, as a reminder, you're using a pitch to simply to get the meeting and once you're in the actual meeting you can use a great consultative approach.

When using your pitch to generate a meeting, you're promising to deliver the solution in the sales meeting. If you said, "I will give you 3 strategies that you can use in your practice over the next 4 weeks to increase cash flow by 38%" it means that your prospect is going into that meeting expecting those strategies. But if all they get are questions because you are using a consultative approach, they'll be pissed. I'll show you how to transition into the consultative approach and ask for permission to go through the exercise so that the prospect has the right expectation. First, let me show you what happens when you try to use a consultative sales approach for every situation just because you've been told that it's the best way to sell.

I received a few emails from a salesperson that wanted to work at MindStorm. In an effort to spare his feelings we'll change his name (to protect the guilty) and just call him Paul. Paul had a great resume with many years of experience in sales, everything from being a million-dollar producer to building and managing teams for the companies he's worked for. Although it was clear from his resume that he had a ton of experience, I passed on hiring Paul based on my personal preference to home grow our salespeople. MindStorm has an incredible sales training program and this allows us to take someone inexperienced and grow them quickly. The finished product is a salesperson specialized in our unique science of selling, without bad habits and baggage from their past.

For over two months I'd been getting an email from Paul every week, and each week I would let Paul know that the answer was no. At first, I'd let him down easy and explained we weren't hiring. After a few more emails I'd fib a little and say that I'd keep him in mind when we were expanding our team. As he got more persistent, it became simpler to just tell Paul the truth (or at least what I thought was the truth) that it was never going to happen. But over time he wore down my resistance and demonstrated that he could handle rejection. Full disclosure, some of my responses towards the end would have sent the average person to buy a self-help book on rebuilding confidence, get a few hugs from a loved one, and participate in at least three sessions of therapy! Paul would respond with things like, he appreciated how I felt and understood why I would think that way. He also brought additional insight and information to the table that would justify me to reconsider my decision. How he handled objections was beautiful.

I finally gave Paul the okay on one condition; he'd start out as a prospector and then move to the full sales position. If he demonstrated that he could do well as a prospector, then the move to sales would happen quickly. But he couldn't get out of the prospecting position until he was successful at it. This is the first snag we hit with Paul, because throughout his entire career every company made him responsible for prospecting, selling, and managing those accounts. As you can appreciate, these are three completely different roles, and the most successful sales organizations operate like an assembly line, with a strong focus on each one. By combining these tasks into one role, you have a team of generalists and nobody becomes great at any one of those tasks. That in turn means your salesperson sucks at getting leads, can't close, and is a terrible account manager for your clients.

Paul just couldn't get his head wrapped around all this. "So, I'm going to have to prospect all day?" he asked. No Paul, you're going to have to prospect all month. How else are you going to get good at it? How else will you understand the importance of it when we recommend the same set up to a client? If you don't believe in it, and you obviously don't, then how can you sell it? This was my point in making Paul start out prospecting. It wasn't to demote him or make him prove himself, it was simply a training strategy to get him acclimated to our world. There have been many advances in the science of selling since Paul had started his career, and this was the very reason for my reluctance in hiring him in the first place.

Now let's go back to my earlier point about consultative selling. One time we sent out a cold email campaign to a targeted list of prospects, and the email read:

> Hi {first name}, I noticed... {insert personalization about the company}.
>
> I have an idea that can double your sales pipeline in 90 days and it will take me less than 15 minutes to explain it in detail. We've already helped dozens of companies like X, Y, and Z do the same. Can I share it with you? It's pretty amazing!

We've gotten good responses from these simple, almost silly emails. I wouldn't try to use this as a template since this was used a few years back and today it wouldn't do as well. The more people do something the more competitive things get and the better you must be to stand out. This book will show you timeless principles for consistently creating great campaigns, but first, back to a conversation that didn't go as well with our buddy Paul. A prospect responded and was eager to hear the strategy. The conversation between Paul and the prospect went like this:

Paul: *Hi Philip, this is Paul from MindStorm. You just responded to my email.*

Phillip: *Oh yes, hi Paul. I have a few minutes before my meeting. So, tell me about this idea you had.*

Paul: *Yes definitely, but before I do I'd love to learn more about your business.*

Phillip: *(With hesitation in his voice) Okay, well ah... we are a logistics company. I've owned the company for the last 21 years and we've been steady. No increase in business, no decrease. It's been even for the last few years, and now that I have my son involved we are looking to grow it. So, you mentioned that you had an idea on how I can increase my sales. I'd love to hear it.*

Paul: *Yes, it's just that for me to determine how to help you, I need to get a better understanding of your business. I'd like to go over things like: What are you doing now to get business? What have you tried in the past? What has and has not worked for you before? Are you looking for a done-for-you service or something you would implement in house?*

Phillip: *I'm looking to grow my business. Look, I took this call because you emailed me and said you had an idea and it would take only a few minutes to share it, so I was open to hear it. Now I find out that you have no idea and you want to ask me all these questions, for what? So, you can figure it out? What is this supposed to be some kind of brainstorming session? I appreciate the effort, but I have a meeting in a couple of minutes, so we'll just have to do this some other time.*

This is a prime example of why the consultative approach is not fit for every occasion. In this case Phillip is expected to be given information, not spend the entire time giving information. Think of the audacity in asking, "Hey can you give me some of your precious time (that you'll never get back) just so I can ask you enough questions to figure out what I can sell you?" In this stage your prospect wants to talk to people that can bring information to the table. This is how I fixed that call:

> **Me:** *Hi Phillip, my name is George Athan and I'm the CEO of MindStorm. I'm sorry to interrupt but I overheard a part of your conversation with Paul and before you go, I just want to give you the strategy we promised you. After that you can decide if you want to continue the dialogue when you have more time, is that fair?*

> **Phillip:** *Yes, I'm always open to ideas but unfortunately, I'm supposed to be on a call in four minutes.*

> **Me:** *Not a problem, I'll deliver it in two. We found that in the last five years competition has risen in your industry.*

> **Phillip:** *It sure has!*

> **Me:** *With all the competition in the marketplace, customers have many more options to choose from. Meanwhile companies are having a hard time differentiating themselves, so everyone is competing on price. Have you had a similar experience in your local market?*

> **Phillip:** *Yes, and I don't want to drop my rates so low that it's not even worth getting the business.*

> **Me:** *You won't have to if you differentiate effectively. What's even worse Phillip, is most companies I speak with do not have a systematic process to acquire new customers. They advertise here*

and there, they spend money on marketing, but they do not have a step by step process that they can repeat over and over to get consistent and predictable results when it comes to getting new accounts. Would you say that's true for your company?

Phillip: *That is 100% true for us and I honestly believe that's our biggest problem.*

Me: *In an effort to respect your time, because I know you have to go, I'll leave you with this. Right now, there are at least 100 companies that are frustrated with their current vendor and need your services.*

Yet, they have no idea that you exist or if they've heard of your company, they have no idea that you're the perfect fit for them and can solve their biggest challenges when it comes to your services. Write this down. What you need to do is:

1. Create a list of your most targeted prospects. Make sure you identify the decision makers and get their all their contact information.
2. Create a message that demonstrates why you're perfect for them. Explain what makes you different from your competitors and why that difference can better solve their challenges. Speak to the frustrations they have which you can solve.
3. Consistently reach out to them using email, LinkedIn, direct mail, and the telephone to set up sales meetings.
4. Train your salespeople or get training on how to turn the meetings into new accounts.

Me: *Phillip, that's what my company does. Although those 4 steps sound simple, we've spent years testing, adjusting, tweaking our methodology down to a science to get you the highest responses possible to grow your business the fastest. We eliminate the* *learning curve, set up the entire system for you, and train your team how to perfect it so you have a process that brings in new accounts each and every month. If this sounds interesting to you then we can set a meeting where we can go into more detail and show you what this process has done for companies similar to yours, and specifically what it would look like for you. Would you like that?*

In less than 4 minutes I was able to demonstrate that I didn't need his information to offer a strategy that solved his problem, because I already knew what his problem was. At least I assumed I knew. We specifically created a prospecting campaign to sell the service I described above, which means if he didn't need a systematic way to get new clients then I would immediately find out that this was not a good prospect for us. Think of prospecting in the sense of prospecting for gold. The goal is to find gold, not find copper and try to convert it to gold. We know copper can never be converted to gold, yet we lie to ourselves and pretend it's a possibility. We're just as seduced by the idea today as they were with alchemy in medieval times. But the reality is, it's either gold or it's not. If it isn't gold, we move on and keep prospecting.

The main lesson here was that the consultative approach was best used at the face-to-face meeting we secured later. At that point the prospect had already committed to giving us more time, allowing us to dig deeper so we can get into more detail of how this solution would fit into their world. But he only gave us the time for a deeper discovery session after he liked our initial pitch. He liked the pitch because we came with solutions first, questions later. What we came to the table with, demonstrated that we wouldn't waste his time. Every step of your process, sells the value of taking the next step.

The secondary lesson is that people often try to make things work and take on clients that aren't a perfect fit just because they don't want to turn the opportunity down. I see companies make this mistake all the time and I will tell you that taking on clients that aren't a good fit often leads to dissatisfied customers. This often precedes damage to your reputation, customer attrition, and less profit. As I said, every time someone in your company is required to communicate with a customer over a completed transaction, it makes that transaction less profitable. More resources are being put into a transaction that wasn't the right fit in the first place and often that transaction ultimately gets reversed. Imagine throwing more resources towards a transaction that you refunded and never get paid on. Not only is this transaction unprofitable, but it becomes an expense eating your other profits.

Even the most positive of circumstances would lead to this transaction slowing you down. Let's say you took on a project that was outside your wheelhouse and you made it a success. The cost here was time because any new territory that you're in reduces your speed and speed is a major component to growth. You're better off finding either a new prospect or finding if this prospect's need can be met with another product or service that is in your wheelhouse. Resist the urge to 'make it work'.

Resource: If you'd like a copy of the latest cold email templates we use, just go to www.client-machine.com/coldemail

Prospecting

Many different terms have been used to describe the prospecting process; cold calling, telemarketing, cold email and social selling, to name a few. Leads can be generated many ways, and just like an acupuncturist suggesting acupuncture while a surgeon recommends surgery, I will offer you my go-to strategy for systematically generating high-quality meetings. Unless you have a defined process, you don't have a *system* at all. That process must be repeatable and produce consistent results so that you can create predictable revenue. If we can predict something, we can plan for it. If we can plan, then we can be proactive and take action. Having this kind of control over generating clients and producing sales is vital for rapid growth. Without it, you have a lot of uncertainty, just hoping for the best, always reacting to things you weren't prepared for. You can imagine how slowly you'd have to move to operate under these conditions.

That term *Predictable Revenue* was popularized by Aaron Ross in his book of the same name. He tells the story of how, in 2002, he helped Salesforce.com add over $100M in revenue by using cold email to generate leads for the sales team. With the success of his book, Aaron paved the way for the modern marketer, as now most sales-savvy companies routinely use, or are considering using, cold email in their prospecting process. Just like everything else, this is getting saturated too. The success Aaron had in 2002 with his innovative approach is different to what people are experiencing today, because at that time no one else was really doing it. At the very least, it's safe to say that no one was doing it as systematically, while scaling and doing the volume Salesforce.com had done at the time. Today, cold email is a common practice and technology is making it easier to systemize this process. In fact, it's becoming such a common practice that new companies are being created just to provide their cold email software to the market. What does this mean for you? This means that cold email prospecting will become just as common as a cold call, a direct mail letter, and any other commonly used vehicle to prospect.

My prediction is that email will be overused until it's not effective at all or until the CAN-SPAM Act of 2003 is updated to eliminate this practice all together. I hope I'm completely wrong in this prediction, but we've already seen a ban on it in Canada. The reason I'm so confident in my prediction is that there are many benefits to using email for prospecting that other vehicles cannot compete with, which in turn will create the overuse. Let's start with price. Compare sending 5,000 emails and mailing 5,000 letters. The emails can be sent out at almost $0 cost and the letters can cost up to $5,000 when you factor in postage, paper, ink, and manpower. Cost alone would force many small businesses to choose email over direct mail. Let's compare it to telephone calls that would also have a $0 cost to deliver. First, the time involved for an employee to make 5000 calls will not be $0, so email is cheaper.

But the biggest advantage email has over telemarketing is the 'no rejection' factor. Of course, people can respond negatively to your email campaigns, but most salespeople would choose to avoid talking to people who might have something negative to say. With email, it's easy to delete the NO's and focus on calling back the people who responded positively. With current technology, email is the easiest form of prospecting and it's the cheapest, and without the rejection. Easier, cheaper, and more pleasant is the ultimate cocktail mix for the number one most highly used practice. Some executives already get 300-400 emails a day in their inbox, so over time with overuse, this method becomes less effective. As that happens, people tend to resort to the numbers game mentality, doing more volume, again creating a perpetual spiral until this wonderful vehicle is destroyed completely.

In an effort to save cold email from its death, I'd like to teach you how to do it effectively so that the practice stays around as long as possible. Cold email is an amazing way to bypass the gatekeeper and communicate directly with a hard-to-reach executive. But choosing to send cold email without taking the time to learn best practices, you are participating in the extinction of a tool that, if correctly used, could consistently generate millions of dollars in sales each year for you.

Cold Email Basics:

Keep them short: Nobody wants to read a novel from someone they don't know and I can say with confidence that nobody is interested in reading a novel over email, period, regardless who it comes from! Plus, most executives read email from their mobile phone. These screens are much smaller than computers, making it even harder and less interesting to read a long email. Lose the introduction. They can find your name and title at the signature on the bottom of your email if it's interesting enough to read that far. This saves an entire sentence. Keep it short and to the point.

Exercise: Imagine you'll get paid for every word you eliminate from your email. Do this with every cold email you write. People respond to very brief emails.

Personalize: We've spoken at length about the problem of mass marketing, and using general language. Your target prospect isn't fooled anymore just because the software you use filled in his first name. Instead of creating a huge list and speaking to everyone at the same time, write one personal email and think about how that can be sent to more people. It sounds the same but it's not. The same technology that allows you to insert their first name, also has the capability of inserting other inputs. For example; pretend you found 50 software companies in the fintech space that you feel would be a perfect fit for you service. During your research, you went to their blog and copied the title of a blogpost written by the executive you're targeting. This information can be loaded right into your email software and as 50 emails go out, you can reference 50 different blog posts in your email campaign. This is just the beginning, because personalization should go far beyond this. You should have different 'snippets' of information that is personal to that prospect. Personalize as often as you can, showing you know a lot of information about them. This tells your prospect that you've done your homework and you already know it's a fit, so they shouldn't disregard your message.

You don't matter, they do: Fight the urge to use I, We, Me, Our Company, or your company's name. Meanwhile, they love reading their name, they love seeing their company's name, they love hearing the name of their products, they love talking about themselves. Your prospect is the only one that matters in that conversation - at least to the prospect. This is true in life as well. People don't even realize how much they love to talk about themselves, so when you ask them a question giving them another opportunity to talk about themselves, they just eat it up. You want your language to light them up inside and if you make every sentence about them you will be moving that emotional needle in your favor.

> **Side Note:** Do not lose authority in doing so. If you act like a gushing superfan, you will lose respect from the person you're trying to connect with. Come from your power.

Don't try to sell: This may seem counterintuitive, but your goal is not to sell. Your goal is to create interest in having a conversation with you at a later time to see if there may be a fit between the two companies. If you can't create interest, it's better to pique their curiosity rather than try to go long form and sell. Ever get those long IT emails from offshore developers trying to tell you about every service they can offer? You've seen the email before. It gives you the different rates for developers and project managers, tells you about all the different platforms they work on, and even give examples of sample projects. Besides the fact that they're randomly sending emails to anyone (spam), they think that you'll just read a sales pitch over email and miraculously be sold. Rule one, keep them short. Rule four, don't sell. You'll get a better response if you briefly ask if your topic is something they'd like to have a conversation about. The goal is positive responses at this stage.

Use email just to get them to engage: Whether you get a positive response or a negative one, your response should always be to transition from email to the telephone. The reason for this is simply, you'll get further on the telephone than you will over email. Once the prospect engages, it's no longer a cold call. The prospect has heard of your company, knows of its offering, and by responding has directly sent you an email. There is nothing cold about this call. In fact, when calling back, often you have a direct number or extension because it was on the prospects signature at the bottom of the email. The newly formed relationship you have with the prospect is enough to get you past gatekeepers. When the gatekeepers ask you what the call is in reference to, simply respond with, "It's regarding the email he sent me a few minutes ago. Can you mention George Athan is on the phone? Thanks." Works every time.

I'll give you a telephone script that you can use to turn around 'NO' responses roughly 20% - 25% of the time. What's great about transitioning to the telephone is that it's an opportunity to take the relationship further by using a more intimate form of contact. For example, what would you feel more obligated to respond to? A letter in the mail or an email sent to you personally? How about responding to an email or answering my question while we were on the telephone? One last scenario: Is it easier to hang up on me or throw me out of your office? This is why email (done right) gets more responses than direct mail, telephone (done right) gets more responses than email, and face-to-face meetings (done right) get a better response than the telephone. The same way it may not be efficient to go door to door cold because setting an appointment up over the phone first would make more sense, it wouldn't make sense making call after call cold when you can wait to speak to the people who were willing to engage with you first. Trust me, if someone doesn't even have the interest, courtesy, or enough respect for you to give you a response, there is zero chance of them buying from you. At least at this stage.

Chapter 6

The Whole Greater Than the Sum of its Parts

Secret Breakthrough in Prospecting?

From time to time people get excited about a new tool that's going to be the game changer in their business. It can be a piece of software that's going to generate an abundance of leads, a magic script that's going to get your prospects to say YES or a specific approach that will do all the above. Although these are marketed as stand-alone systems, each one of these represents a core component of outbound lead generation. By understanding what these components are, you can optimize each part and incorporate all of them into your campaign to compound your results. At that point it becomes only a matter of documenting each step to standardize a process for your organization and make sure that it is followed by all, every time. The core components of outbound marketing are:

- **Target**
- **Vehicle**
- **Message**
- **Offer/Value/Bribe**
- **Cadence**
- **# of Follow-Ups**
- **Automation Tools**
- **The Process/Workflow**

After the success of Aaron Ross' book *Predictable Revenue*, 'cold email' became the next miracle in the eyes of salespeople and small business owners all over the country. Emails would be sent en masse, without a strategy in place or a good understanding of the fundamentals behind successful campaigns. These initiatives were launched with only the excitement of potential sales to support them. Naturally, when people didn't get the results they had read about and hoped for, a demand opened in the market. Bryan Kreuzberger's *Breakthrough Email System* came at the perfect time, offering salespeople an email template that promised to get 60-80% response rates. By now you've most likely received an email using a variation of Bryan's template, also known as the 'Appropriate Person' email. Bryan had great success marketing his *Breakthrough Email System* because it helped salespeople create structure in their writing and process to follow. The truth is that both Aaron's and Bryan's teachings included all the components above, which means they were in fact end-to-end processes. Did Aaron have a template for everyone to follow? Yes. Did Bryan follow up process to supplement the email template? Yes. But they focused on the one component the market needed most: Aaron made a new prospecting vehicle popular with 'cold email' which would replace cold calling and Bryan showed the importance of the message with his wildly popular 'Appropriate Person' template. Bryan did such a great job bringing awareness to how important the message is that salespeople started searching the internet for other email templates to use.

The truth is that every component is important. There's not one that's so important that you can disregard all the others. Let's go through each component to ensure you build lead generation machines that pump out meetings for you.

Target: We've already covered in detail the importance of your target. This is where you're creating your ideal client profile, your buyer personas, and building your highly-targeted list. Your target is the most important component to your campaign. If you were selling steaks to a list of Vegans, you probably wouldn't do so well. Your goal is target the prospects that would be a perfect fit for your product or service, making the decision to respond an obvious one. Find the people or companies you can add the most value to, and have the greatest impact on. If you can't solve their problem or you can't help them, they won't respond to your messaging and they won't become your next client. Although this is bad, I'll tell you what would be even worse. Targeting someone whose problem you couldn't effectively solve, someone you won't be able to deliver for, and they do become your client. That would be a nightmare.

Best Practice: Instead of the waterboard approach of pouring all your efforts onto just one individual in the organization, I recommend the top-down waterfall approach of reaching out to multiple decision makers in the organization. If you don't get the response you were hoping for from one individual, you still have other irons on the fire at that company. This will dramatically increase your responses. The reason for the top-down approach of reaching out to higher level executives is also recommended because you will often get bunted down to the person that is responsible for handling that task. When you reach out to that individual and explain that their boss's boss suggested you meet with them, that becomes a relatively easy meeting to get. On the other hand, attempting to do this in reverse and telling a higher-level executive that they should meet with you because a lower level employee suggested so, will not nearly have the same effect.

Vehicle: We have many different delivery vehicles to choose from, and deciding which to use often depends on the size and complexity of your sale. If you are trying to generate leads to reach small business owners, it can be as simple as only using cold email or LinkedIn for prospecting. If you're trying to get meetings with C-Suite executives of large corporations, you may have to use a combination of those, plus direct mail, telephone, digital marketing, and even singing telegram. I'm not suggesting the last one but the more you touch your prospect using different vehicles, the better your chances of achieving awareness. This is the first stage of the **AIDA Model: Awareness, Interest, Desire, Action.**

Even with all the excitement surrounding cold email, the reality is it's just another vehicle. At one point, direct mail was the go-to vehicle until that became oversaturated and the term 'junk mail' was born. Cold calling was all the rage until people got tired of 'telemarketing calls'. Just as quickly, cold email is being abused and, just like fifteen years ago, more and more people are talking about getting spam. At MindStorm, not only do we incorporate cold email into all our clients' campaigns, but we also use LinkedIn in a specific way to prospect, because executives that are on LinkedIn hardly get any other messages in their InMail box. As an added bonus, LinkedIn also sends an email copy of the message to the user with almost 100% deliverability to their inbox.

Best Practice: Contact your prospect using multiple vehicles. Consider both the value of the meeting and the potential profit from the sale and adjust your spend accordingly. For big ticket sales and high value meetings, consider adding 3-Dimensional mailings to your campaign. These are physical items being delivered, which require uncommon mailing packaging. Sending someone a **FedEx** package will have a completely different effect, thus response rate, than sending a regular envelope, even when the exact same letter is inside. Start with easier and cheaper vehicles and then escalate to more expensive, attention-grabbing methods over time and touches. This will enable you to capture the low hanging fruit and secure many meetings at a lower cost per lead. This is an important strategy considering we are building a system that we will scale to manage volume.

Message: When we're talking about the message, we're talking about the language used to communicate with a prospect. This can be everything from the copywriting of your landing pages or direct mail letters, to the telephone scripts your salespeople use. The message is what connects the benefit of your product to the target audience you're reaching out to. This is another vital component to your lead generation process because regardless of the vehicle you're using to connect with a prospect, without the right message you'll never move them through the next phases of the AIDA Model - Creating **I**nterest and **D**esire for your services, eventually getting your prospect to **A**ct.

When we talk about systems, we mean processes that can be repeated to get predictable results. To achieve this, certain things have to be constant so that they produce results that are consistent and therefore can be relied on. One of these constants is the message. How can you predict with certainty the outcome of a campaign if the message changed every time? You couldn't. The more variables that you make constant, the more you can rely on your expectation of the results. Even yet, with all things being the same every time, responses change because people change. What works today will not necessarily work tomorrow. With this much uncertainty and constantly moving targets, it would be impossible to generate predictable results with a different message each time.

Direct Mail: An entire book could be written on the topic of 'The Message'. Specific courses are dedicated to copywriting, while others deal with how to create the best scripts. We covered some basics earlier on how to craft cold emails, and I would add that when it comes to direct mail, you can do very well with long-form letters. Each word is an opportunity to create excitement in your prospect, so your goal is to use as many as you can. Make it easy to read by breaking up the text into short paragraphs, and separate headers with bold print. This tells the prospect how much of your wording to consume at one time. When your paragraph is complete, and your point is made, they can stop and absorb the information as opposed to choking on it. You want to make it as easy as possible to read by making it visually appealing. Use headers, small paragraphs, bullet points, and even graphics.

Benefit Statement: A benefit statement tells the prospect immediately what you can do for them and why that's important. It's specific to the audience you're targeting, the challenges they have, and the solution you're offering to solve the problem. The power behind the benefit statement is that it either creates curiosity or interest within the few-second window a prospect gives you to determine if something is worthy of their time, or it allows the individual to immediately identify that this is not what they are in the market for. In the latter, getting a NO is just as important as getting a YES because it saves you the time that can be better spent on finding and following up with real prospects. It's when you get no response that you have a problem. You can spend weeks of your life chasing people that were never going to have any interest.

For example, if we are reaching out to VP's to have a conversation about our Ultimate Prospector product and service suite, the benefit statement may be:

> We help {blank} companies rapidly increase sales. MindStorm uses breakthrough methods in prospecting that can double your current sales pipeline in 90 days. In fact, 80% of the process is automated so your sales team can focus on closing deals.

Context is everything, so it's important to know that you don't just stamp your benefit statement on anything and everything, expecting it to magically produce customers. However, this should be used in all your communications in some form to help the prospect you're touching to understand the value you bring to the table, and the problems you solve. Your benefit statement is a mini-USP (unique sales proposition), your USP is a mini-elevator pitch, your elevator pitch is a mini-presentation, and your presentation is just one component of your entire sales pitch.

Telephone Scripts: There's a debate amongst sales gurus on whether to use telephone scripts or not. To me, this is not even a debate. We can't expect anyone to produce an optimal result without giving them a structure to follow, a structure that we methodically create in advance. Can they produce that result just by winging it? Sure. Will they produce that every time? Absolutely not. So why would we want to build a system that we plan on scaling, when we know it's flawed? This would only multiply your losses. Messages are vital in all areas, not just sales. Imagine if your customer service people were responding to customers using a different language in every scenario. Knowing that their responses are influenced by their own emotional state, who knows exactly what they can and can't say on the company's behalf to a difficult customer. I know some of you reading this don't currently have a 'system' in place for how to handle each response in your customer service process and this is a gentle reminder to create one. A script is just a mini-system.

Best Practice: Control as much communication as possible. Write out every possible telephone script, email message, voicemail message, LinkedIn message and letter written on your company's behalf. This should go for every department in the company, but at the very least start with sales. Have standardized communication templates that feel personal, but systematically dictate how you or your employees will interact with prospects and customers. In sales, anticipate every possible response your prospect might and will say. Carefully think about the best possible words that should be said in that precise moment and train your salespeople on them often. This way, when the time comes, and your prospect has a concern, that concern is addressed in the best possible way with the best possible response. Since everyone will be trained on this, they will be able to deliver that response with precision timing and perfect delivery. I heard persuasion expert Scott Sylvan Bell once say, "Sales is a performance". Not only do I believe that statement, but nothing can describe my view any better.

Offer/value: You've targeted the right people, you've used different vehicles to capture their attention, and your messaging piqued their interest. Your offer, and the value it has, will be the deciding factor in whether your prospect says YES or NO. In fact, your offer has even more impact than your actual messaging. You can write bad copy but give an offer they can't refuse, and you'll often get a YES response. You can write excellent copy but give an offer they have absolutely no interest in, the answer will almost always be NO. If your offer is more important than your messaging, than why are we listing this later? Because if you make mistakes structuring your messages and scripts, your prospect will never have the opportunity to get to your offer. They'll throw away your 'junk mail', delete your 'spam email', or hang up on your 'telemarketing call' before you get the opportunity to make your offer. Obviously, you're not sending junk and your call has much more value than a telemarketing call, but with bad messaging your prospect doesn't know that.

Let's take a look at what different offers feel like on the receiving end, and maybe it will give some insight into the feelings you might be creating for prospects in your campaigns. Say you're the CEO of a fast-growing tech company. As sales are increasing and money is being thrown around during your expansion, you start to feel as if you've outgrown the financial people around you and you're now looking to find experts that can understand the complexity of your business so that you're not throwing more money away, or overpaying in taxes. There's a company that targeted you because of your growth and they've positioned themselves as the go-to experts in their messaging. Under these circumstances, which offer feels more enticing?

Offer 1: A free consultation.

Offer 2: Strategy session with Expert John Smith to show you how a tax structure like Google's Double Irish can be legally applied to your business.

Given the scenario, maybe you'd go for both offers because the company did a great job targeting and messaging, identifying someone with a huge need. But some of your campaigns won't be so obvious to your prospect. Not everyone is going to be in the market or looking for your services in the way we created in this convenient example. Either way, the second offer is much more compelling and will always get more responses. Decades ago a smart individual thought of the phrase 'free consultation' and reframed a sales pitch to sound like people were getting free consulting. Just like anything else, when something becomes overused it no longer has the same effect. Today, the phrase free consultation is understood to be an obvious sales pitch.

One of my clients sells a great product to veterinarian practices. The challenge his salespeople have had through the years is that these vets are so busy, they don't have time to meet with or speak to a salesperson. When I was talking about using direct outreach to get appointments with the vets, across the board, the sales team told me it would be impossible. I almost always get this response the first time working with salespeople who target hard-to-reach prospects. They consistently remind me that their industry is different and that they can't even get veterinarians on the telephone, much less getting a few minutes of their time in person. I explained that people make time for things they find valuable. And the only reason they haven't gotten these vets to make time for them, is because they aren't offering enough value in exchange for that time.

So in response, we created a Lunch & Learn where we catered in for the whole practice, while my client's team would share the latest research in digestive issues found in the performance horses those practices treat. The presentation delivered the value it promised, and it highlighted some of the problems that have not been addressed in the industry. This allowed the vets to talk about the challenges they experience, and more importantly, it created the opportunity to discuss my client's products that solved those issues. The salespeople had a chance to see that the same vets who previously wouldn't give them a minute of their time, had now given them more than hour, and in some cases two! Not only that, but we weren't just talking about one vet that the sales team had trouble getting time with. These practices were stopping everything they were doing, and all their vets were participating. By creating enough value around the offer, they now had a captive audience fully engaged in their message.

Best Practice: Make a list of offers you can extend that would be perceived as high value. Is there a problem you can solve or a service you'd be willing to provide at no cost? Can you give a free trial of your product? Think about different ways you can build that relationship. Remember, it's not always about moving the purchase forward. Sometimes it's more about moving the relationship forward and the purchase will come after. Is there someone you can introduce your prospect to that they might find high value? Can you give them some other access? What can you teach? A good strategy is to offer your prospect information on how to solve their problem. This can be a webinar, one-on-one session, or even an event like the Lunch & Learn or a free seminar. The bigger your offer, the higher the response. As long as you deliver what you promise in that offer, there's nothing wrong with adding a sales pitch in your presentation. In fact, your information is your sales pitch. I always believe in making your sales pitch so valuable that your prospects would be willing to pay for it.

Exercise: Brainstorm with your team and have everyone individually make a long list of every possible offer you can make. There are no bad ideas at this stage. Just get everything down on paper. Have each person read their list and discuss how each idea can work. Do not talk about how ideas won't work unless you introduce a solution to the problem you are identifying. While each person goes through their list, everyone else should write down one or two of the best ideas they hear during the exercise. The final stage is to have each person present the best idea (two at most) that they've heard with their own spin on it. At the end of this exercise you may have 5-7 great offers that you can use in your campaigns. You can regularly approach your prospects with different offers. If someone doesn't find one offer valuable, they may respond to another. Track your efforts to see what offers get the highest response.

# of Follow Ups: In sales, the fortune is in the follow up. There's more opportunity lost by salespeople not having a good follow up strategy, than through anything else. I use the word strategy because that would assume you have a consistent protocol for following up. When it comes to prospecting, having a follow-up strategy becomes especially important because your response rates are much lower reaching out cold to strangers. It's obvious that if you've built a relationship with a prospect, they're more likely to reply to your emails or return your phone calls than someone that you have absolutely no relationship with. To compensate for this fact, often your contact efforts may have to be more audacious in nature to grab attention and more 'touches' are required before you get a response.

If you were manually following up with different names on a list, making some calls here and sending some emails there, you would probably be distributing your efforts unevenly, with one prospect reached out to seven times and another one only contacted twice. What if the bigger opportunity was the one that you only reached out to twice, while the person you reached out to seven times had no ability to buy from you at all? This can easily happen because, until you speak to the prospect and qualify them, you *don't actually know* who is who. The goal is to systematically distribute your efforts, not evenly, but relative to the opportunity. The biggest opportunities should obviously be given more effort, while limiting your efforts on the smaller opportunities. When trying to get a meeting with a CEO of a large corporation, it's understandable you'd spend an enormous amount of time, energy, and money trying to get that appointment, as long as getting the sale would justify that expense. But what if you have an average size sale and you had the wrong contact information for this individual? A telephone number that goes straight to voicemail, an old email address where he never gets the message, or you're calling a gatekeeper that will never let you through? So much wasted time and energy.

When considering your follow-up strategy, consider the effort required and its relative effectiveness. If you reach out too little and give up too early, you lose the opportunity that prospect offers. If you reach out too much and put more effort than is worth doing business with that person, then the opportunity cost is in the time lost in not reaching out to other prospects that are more reachable. When it comes to email and automation, this doesn't necessarily apply. You can load 50 message templates in an automation software and let automation reach out to an empty mailbox for the next two years without you even having to think about it. It's when you are thinking about them, going through your notes in your CRM, and leaving voicemails that eats up your valuable time.

Best Practice: There's no magic number to give you for the perfect number of follow up efforts. This must be custom to your campaign, and calculated considering the opportunity and the effort required. Sometimes some executives with equal buying power are easier to reach than others. Therefore, I recommend reaching out to multiple contacts in the organization. With cold emailing campaigns, we send out a minimum of 8 touches to 3 different people. Remember when you're adding value like we spoke about earlier; more touches equal more benefit.

Side Note: Change the vehicle so it doesn't get annoying, and change the offer to add layers of value. This can be done by using email, direct mail, social media, and leaving voicemails, offering tools, information, free services, jokes, ideas, and more. The more people trying to get your prospect's attention, the more you're going to have to follow up to stand out. Also, it shows that you are committed to speaking to them, that what you have to say is important.

Cadence: Your cadence is your sales pulse, the frequency of your contact efforts. This is also something that should be predetermined in advance. Contact someone too frequently and it can be construed as annoying or too aggressive, contact someone not frequently enough and you may never get a response because the distance between your communications makes the prospect forget about who you are. It's almost like you're starting over and coming in cold for the first time, every time. A good balance will allow your communications to build on each other and establish a relationship over time, without being too much.

Best Practice: Start with a baseline of one email, one voicemail, or one direct mail contact per week when prospecting, and adjust this according to the urgency of the situation. When I say urgency, I'm speaking in the best interest of the prospect or the sale, not yours. In other words, if you were to find out that your prospect was using a trial version of your competitor's product, then it's important to get a hold of them within a couple of days or they might finalize their buying decision before you even had an opportunity to present a better option. What this doesn't mean is that your quarterly quota is on the horizon, so you turn up the intensity. Although this will result in getting more meetings faster, it's not a best practice because you will lose other opportunities overall, just for being too aggressive. When you must get a hold of them immediately and you're forced to contact them numerous times in a short period, I recommend using different vehicles with each contact. The amazing thing is that we can use 3 different vehicles in the same week and it won't feel annoying. But try emailing a cold prospect 3 times in the same week or leave 3 voicemails. It will feel too aggressive. You may get a response, but it won't be the response you want.

At MindStorm, we start cold email campaigns with 8 contacts over 50 days. We start with contact every 5 days and then lower the frequency after a few touches. Be careful contacting someone every 7 days, as this will always have you reaching out to your prospect on the same day of the week. Many executives have set schedules for consistency and you may always be reaching out on a day that's never convenient. And thinking that you'll just send an email or leave a voicemail and expecting a busy prospect to call you back on a day that is more convenient for them is just unrealistic.

Automation Tools: This is a very important component in scaling your lead generation efforts. If we want fast growth, we need to shave minutes off every process used by every person. These minutes can be reinvested in high ROI activities, such as acquiring new clients or generating more revenue. One of the added benefits of using email in your prospecting is the abundance of software tools that support the activity. For complex sales that would benefit from using multiple vehicles, there are printing and mailing services that can integrate with your CRM, as well as marketing automation software. Whether you only need to send a postcard, or you want to send a shoebox container filled with surprises, you have the ability to incorporate a variety of customized direct mail pieces in a sophisticated workflow where it can be automated and scaled.

In order to help you understand these principles, it wouldn't make sense to name too many specific products or companies, as these things change too often. What we consider great at the time of this writing will become old news very shortly. The important thing is to understand that the more you can automate, the less you need to rely on people. Apart from the occasional bugs, software will do what you ask, when you ask it to, every time. Although nothing can replace the value people provide, we as humans also have our weaknesses. Software can't represent the emotions or the limiting beliefs that often get in our way. Have you ever second-guessed calling someone or sending an email? Software doesn't second guess anything, it simply does what you ask it to do. Software becomes your employee you can delegate the tasks that are not worth yours or your salespeople's time. Not only is this employee very helpful, they're much cheaper. And, you don't have to worry about health benefits, 401k, or sick days!

Best Practice: Look for tools that integrate with each other. Many stand-alone systems were created as a result of the market moving towards the creation of individual components and away from all-in-one systems. In the past, you had to purchase large cable packages for movie channels, whereas today you can just buy a subscription to HBO Go without even needing to purchase cable. The same thing has happened in software where you can just purchase the one independent piece that you need from a vendor without having to purchase a bundle of their products or services. Instead of purchasing an expensive suite of products that consists of a CRM, dialer, and email automation, you can just choose the one tool you need. Even these products are moving away from the illusion of appealing to mass and they're getting specific, focusing on solving one problem at a time.

Although there are obvious benefits to being able to choose products a la carte, too many independent pieces and moving parts can be challenging when you need them to work together. Integration platforms like Zapier make it easy to connect apps so you can build a workflow using all your favorite tools. There are many integration platform-as-a-service providers (iPaaS) that allow you to connect any combination of processes, services, applications, and data within your organization. Start looking for applications that you can connect. Not only will this simplify your life, but it will also make your campaigns more effective.

The Entire Process/Workflow: As we can see, each piece of the puzzle is vital, as getting just one component wrong can hurt your campaign. Even more vital to your success is how you put all these pieces together. Do you choose email, cold call, or direct mail? How about all three? Should LinkedIn be added and if so, how? In what sequence? The higher the complexity of your sale, the more sophistication required in your process. The opposite is true as well. Many products or services can be sold just using one vehicle alone and automating that process. It's important to understand that you can easily get bogged down by having too many unnecessary steps in your process. The goal is to speed sales through your process, so it stands to reason that having a more complex workflow than needed will only serve to detract from selling activity. There's a delicate balance between efficiency and effectiveness.

A good strategy is to start with one vehicle and see if that alone will do the job, then add accordingly. In choosing which vehicle to use, I always recommend starting with the one that requires the smallest investment of time, money, and energy. In the United States, at the time of writing, cold email is that vehicle. For my friends in Canada, this practice was banned in July 2014 where the law now prohibits unsolicited messages even to social media accounts, which effectively eliminates social selling, so be sure to check the rules and regulations in your country to stay compliant. Assuming that you can use email in your prospecting, the question is, do you continue using that same vehicle in your follow ups or do you follow up the email with a telephone call for example? That answer to that depends on a few things. If you can serve 28 million businesses and you have only two sales people, I'd say just keep using the one vehicle because the conversion rate isn't the most important thing here - it's sales. I know that sounds a little like the numbers game mentality that I despise, but the truth is with so much opportunity, telephone calls to prospects that have showed no indication of interest yet would be a very expensive use of your time. On the other hand, if you or your team is going after enterprise clients in a territory with only 50 companies you can target, conversion becomes the most important thing and a sophisticated workflow is required.

The workflow we're discussing in the prospecting process is just to get your prospect to engage with you. Once they respond, sales conversations are happening and this prospect either moves in the direction of becoming a real opportunity or the file is closed. Closing the file means you're no longer contacting them (at least for a period of time) and you're moving on to others who may have interest. With that said, you're building a workflow with the primary goal of capturing attention, creating interest, and getting the prospect to act in the way of having a sales conversation. Your secondary goal is to accomplish all the above with the least amount of time, money, and effort. So, on that basis, how does sequence fit into all this? Does it even matter? It matters enough that your outreach efforts don't feel like completely random acts of contact, but not enough to believe that a magic formula exists that will produce ground breaking results over another method.

I say that with one exception. Sending a letter first and following up with a call, will perform better than making a call first, and sending a letter to follow up. The reason for this is two-fold: First, your call would be cold, which does not get the best response. In fact, a call should never be the first vehicle used to introduce yourself and your offer. Using other vehicles allows the prospect to read your communication in their own time and digest the information you deliver. If you were to do the traditional cold call, you'd most likely reach them at an inconvenient time. Most target prospects, especially high value ones will be in the middle of something else when you reach them, meaning they'll have little attention to allocate to you or your offering. And in order for them to *make* time for you, they would have to already understand the value of speaking with you.

Similarly, letters also don't provide a good mechanism for the prospect to respond to you. A prospect can easily reply to an email but if you send a direct mail piece, they have to take the step of calling you back, which requires more effort and commitment on their part. The reverse order solves both problems because you are not expecting a response from your letter by sending it first, you're sending it to warm up your call.

Best Practice: Start with the vehicles that are less invasive and require the smallest commitment of your prospect's time, and then escalate. For example, say you had a small number of high value prospects that you could target, requiring you to use many different vehicles and many touches. You could start with social media, move to email, follow up with direct mail, speak to on the telephone, then ask to meet in person. Let's use that example to go even deeper:

1. Follow them on Twitter.
2. Retweet or favorite their tweet.
3. @ or mention them in regard to the tweet.
4. Send a LinkedIn connection request with personalized message referencing Twitter engagement.

---

5. After s/he connects, send relationship building welcome message (no soliciting).
6. Like or comment on their LinkedIn post.
7. Send email offering value, asking to speak on the telephone briefly.
8. Follow up with a letter offering even more value if no response.
9. Follow up with a telephone call.
10. Arrange in-person meeting to discuss telephone conversation in more detail.

Each contact justifies the next course of action. A relationship is being built over time and if value is being added, you'll eventually pierce through and get this prospect's attention. Whether or not you create interest will be determined by how accurate you were in your targeting and how compelling your offer is. You can see how starting with Twitter follows can be a complete waste of time if the person you're trying to reach is the purchasing manager of a small company. This overkill can waste precious time when you could have easily gotten the job done with an email. You can also see why people were getting so much resistance when they were cold calling hard-to-reach executives (which is number 9 in the above example) or even worse, field reps just showing up to the prospect's office without ever establishing a relationship prior to that. In the modern sales environment, the traveling field rep cold calling in person has almost entirely disappeared. Hopefully this illustrates why that practice died.

Putting It All Together to Design Your Process

Target the right Prospects: Find the companies that will be the best fit for your product or service. Start with the ones that you can have the biggest impact on, and out of those, are the biggest opportunities for you. Next, target the people that have the authority to say YES. It's better to go top down than to try bottom up. I recommend targeting 3-5 top executives at larger companies and the business owner of smaller companies.

Use the right Vehicles: Start with the easiest and cheapest to use, and only add more if you need them. Don't waste time or money on using too many vehicles, unless you absolutely must. The easiest indicator of the need to escalate is that you are not generating enough leads. But before adding vehicles, first adjust your messages and offers.

Use the right Messaging: Speak directly to the needs of your target prospects and avoid generic speak as often as possible. Use words that ring bells (industry jargon, names, or common phrases used by similar clients) as often as possible. Clearly state the benefits to your prospect and name drop if possible.

Use the right # of Touches: Your follow up should follow two rules: 1) Continue to follow up until you get engagement from the prospect 2) as long as it makes sense for you to. This means that your goal in your emails, LinkedIn messages, direct mail, and telephone calls is to get a response (YES, NO, or maybe). If you don't get a response, you continue as long as you find it to be worth your time.

Use the right Cadence: You can be more aggressive in the beginning, but as your campaign continues, spread your contacts over a larger period. The persistent effort in the beginning is for those who have a need right now and they haven't responded yet because they were busy or haven't seen your offer. This justifies the first few contacts to be delivered in a shorter period. Other than the low-hanging fruit, which represents an average 1-3% of the market that are actively looking for a solution like yours, the rest could be a good fit sometime in the near future. These people haven't said YES to you because they may not have the need or perceive the need in this moment. They haven't said NO to you because they may find value in what you offer and plan to connect with you in the future. If you continue to be aggressive throughout the entire time, you will force these prospects to respond at a time when their only answer can be NO. Keep contacting them for as long as it financially makes sense to, but after the fifth contact I strongly recommend limiting these efforts to every 2-4 weeks so that you stay top of mind without ruining a relationship.

Use the right Offers: As your outreach efforts persist and your vehicles escalate, add more value with each touch. If one offer wasn't compelling enough then increase the intensity by adding more value to future offers, but don't just become more persistent. If the ferocity of your efforts to get in contact surpasses the value in your offering, you will get a response, and the response will be NO.

With the right Workflow: Always attempt to generate leads the simplest way possible so that you're getting the lowest cost per lead (CPL). We're not only talking hard costs, but also time and opportunity costs that can come from adding unnecessary steps to your workflow. Unnecessary steps equal unnecessary money spent. A low CPL is vital when you're scaling because wasted money is multiplied when you scale. At the same time, don't be so consumed in cutting steps that you lose muscle in your mission to shred fat. If you can generate better qualified leads, and in more volume, by adding steps then do so. Just choose the actions that can get you the best results, using the least amount of time, energy, and money. What can you automate or delegate inexpensively?

And that covers the first major objective in your outreach efforts, eliciting a response from your prospect. Without getting the prospect to engage with you, a sale cannot happen and the opportunity to turn the prospect into a client does not exist. In the next chapter we will discuss how to take those responses and turn them into meetings.

Chapter 7

Getting the Meeting

Everything you've done up until this point was to get the attention of your perfect future client, whose challenge you can solve very effectively, and you've created interest within them to have a conversation with you. These actions can be documented for others to follow, and repeated to systematically produce this same result as often as you need it. Now that your prospect is willing to have a conversation with you, it's time to take this small level of interest or this tiny bit of curiosity and turn it into a meeting. By acknowledging that there isn't an overwhelming level of interest at this stage, we can approach the conversation in a way that doesn't require big commitments from your prospect, thereby allowing us to move this relationship forward one step at a time. We can't ask or expect to be given a lot of time at this stage, nor can we expect them to make a buying decision of any kind right now. The goal here is simply to verify that your preliminary research was correct, that they are the best contact you should be speaking with, and that they have a problem that you can solve. The prospect doesn't have to know that they need your help at this stage, as long as they are willing to get into dialogue with you, as the need can be revealed during conversation.

Bridge: Turn Responses into Meetings

In your campaigns, you'll get either positive, negative, or neutral responses to your contact efforts. (We also know that we can get no response at all, and already have a protocol for: continue reaching out until it no longer financially makes sense to). It's important to know what to do or say to turn these responses into a meeting. This is your bridge. Let's discuss the different response groups so that we know how to move them down the path effectively.

Positive Responses: Any time that you get what you ask for (directly or indirectly), you can label this a positive response. If you ask for the name of the person who is responsible for purchasing products like yours and you get a reply with a name or, "I'm the person who handles that," then you had gotten a positive response. If you're asking this person for ten minutes of their time so you can give them a strategy, and the response you get is, "Reach out to me in two weeks," this is also a positive response even though you'd like to speak with them today. The goal is to always be moving the prospect to the next stage and this indication of interest moves you forward.

With positive responses, our goal is to immediately set an appointment for a telephone call so that you can qualify the prospect and set them up for the discovery process. There are numerous ways to receive positive responses from direct response campaigns. Your prospect may have replied to your LinkedIn message or your email, they could have called your office in response to a letter you sent, or even just verbally responded over the telephone during a conversation you were having as you make follow up calls. The vehicle you use to respond is not as important as making sure that the qualifying and discovery calls are done over the telephone or in person. *Do not* have these conversations over email or social media because our goal is to build a relationship with the prospect and move them through each stage of the process as quickly as possible. Trying to have conversations over some type of text will dramatically slow things down as people reply at their convenience. Plus, the telephone is much more intimate than email and face to face is much more intimate than the telephone. This is important because the speed of the relationship moves directly in proportion to the intimacy of your communications. This is always why I recommend getting cell numbers and getting clients comfortable speaking to you on weekends or outside of normal business hours.

Positive Response Asking for Referral: Our top-down approach often tries to get the highest-level executive to engage with us, so they can point us in the right direction of a more appropriate person to speak with. The impact is two-fold. First, it almost forces the lower level employee to take the meeting because it implies the higher-level executive found value in your offering. Second, it gives you access to pull the higher-level executive back into the conversation at any time you need without it feeling like you're going over your prospect's head.

When you get a referral from a higher-level executive, just contact the individual and follow three simple steps for your bridge:

1. Tell them that the CEO (or whatever executive) recommended you speak to them
2. Deliver your benefit statement
3. Ask for a meeting

Hi Bob, your CEO Lisa Smith recommended that I speak with you.

We help software companies double their sales by systematically acquiring enterprise clients, using our breakthrough methodology. For example, we've recently completed a project for Acme Corp, where they captured twenty Fortune 50 clients using our system, ultimately increasing their run rate by $10M.

Since Lisa thought it would be a good idea for us to chat, what day would work best for you?

As I mentioned earlier, it doesn't matter if this was an email, a LinkedIn message, or a telephone call. What matters is that they know someone higher recommended the two of you should speak, that they understand the benefit of speaking with you, and that you ask for a call to take place.

Side Note: If you're not getting a response via email or LinkedIn, move to a call. Also, make sure that you always tell the referring party that you will keep them updated. This gives you the excuse to continue contacting and building a relationship with the high-level executive, and if you are not getting responses from this new contact, you can honestly say that you promised to update their boss on your conversations. Once they realize that they can look bad in the eyes of their superior, usually they become very responsive and a meeting will be set. Remember, this person doesn't know what relationship you have with the high-level executive, but they won't want to take any chances.

If you sell to CEO's then you may get the "I'm the person who handles that" response. In this case, just follow steps two and three:

Hi Bob, it's great to connect with you. I noticed... (insert something personalized). We help... {insert benefit statement that relates to personalization}. When you have a few minutes, I'd like to discuss a strategy we've created for {company name} that can {insert additional benefit}. Do you have a few minutes sometime next week?

Side notes: Don't get caught up on the template because things change. Message templates get overused and become less effective. So, it's best to create your own so that you're the only one using it. I'd also like to bring attention to the seemingly harmless question above. At the close of my response, notice I didn't say something like, "Wednesday at 3pm". When your prospect is reading, or listening to your response, the question in their mind isn't if they have availability on Wednesday at 3pm. It's whether they see enough value in spending time with you on a call, which then may trigger a whole series of future engagements and more time commitments. Right now, their plate is already full, and they can just end this here before it starts, not adding anymore to their busy life. (This serves as a reminder to demonstrate a ton of value in every offering.)

Only once they see the benefit and decide to go forward, do they then ask themselves if Wednesday at 3pm is a good time? By asking them to consider two questions simultaneously, it's almost as if their brain shuts down for the moment, forcing them to spit out the easiest answer possible: NO. We want conversations to be easy and for things to flow from one stage to the next. As this relationship is in the beginning stages, we need to make things as simple as possible for your prospect. Asking them for a lot of time or asking them to think any more than they have to can immediately stop that flow. Make the barrier of entry low for each stage of the process you are transitioning to. By asking questions like, "Do you have a few minutes sometime next week?" it makes it easier to focus on the first implied question "Are you even interested?" without the pressure of the second. Once they have interest in speaking with you, scheduling becomes easy.

Positive Response to Direct Offer: You may get responses like, "Sure, let's talk." This bridge is simple enough; it's just a matter of scheduling. If you're using email or LinkedIn, then I suggest you use an online scheduler. It will integrate with your calendar and give your prospect the ability to choose the day and time that works best for them. Not only will it send them an email to confirm and remind but it can also put the meeting on both of your calendars. Best of all, it makes it much easier than going back and forth over email trying to figure out days and times that work for you both.

It's important that you don't attempt to get into a sales conversation over any type of text: Email, social media, SMS, or messaging apps. Some prospects will attempt to take you off your path and try to take control of your process. We know this can be dangerous. You may hear things like, "Send me information" or, "How much do your services cost?" We know that discussing price before the prospect is even convinced they want or need your service, will most likely kill the sale. We know that just sending information over email will never have the same emotional impact as you personally giving an interactive presentation. This also may end the sale before it even began. Salespeople often give into prospects trying to take control, out of a fear that they'll ruin a relationship and ultimately lose a sale. Out of these two scenarios, there is far more risk giving in and going off the *Speed Path*. Before I discuss what the Speed Path is in detail, let's look at negative and neutral responses.

Neutral Responses: Neutral responses typically come in forms of questions. You see things like, "Do you do X?" or "Do you have Y?" This happens when a prospect has interest, but they are not fully committing to a YES. This may be because they have some reservations, or your exact offering doesn't match what they're looking for. Since these responses are closer to YES than they are to NO, the best course of action is to quickly pick up the phone and call them. What I love about neutral responses is that the prospect already has something in mind that would work for them. For example, in our prospecting campaigns, sometimes we're asked if we would be willing to get paid *after* they see results. This isn't a YES or positive response, because they don't want to bother having a sales conversation about anything that would require them to lay out money. But this isn't a NO or negative response, because they do have interest in the offering. In fact, they already laid out what they're looking for.

The goal is always to move the response to a phone conversation wherever possible. In the example above, we do occasionally allow the right prospects to work on a performance basis, but this is definitely not the norm. In order to determine if they're qualified for the program, we must have a more in-depth conversation in person or over the phone. This wouldn't be something negotiated over email. But, since I can't sell as effectively over email as I can in a live conversation, wouldn't I want to have an in-depth conversation with *every* prospect? Think about it. Even if I can tell that a prospect wouldn't be a fit for our performance-based pricing model, wouldn't I want the opportunity to understand why they're asking for this in the first place? Maybe they're scared we won't perform and I can give them as many references as they needed to feel more comfortable. Maybe they're worried that they don't have the budget because they're assuming our fees are higher than they really are. If I were to just answer their question and tell them NO before having the opportunity to speak with them, we both may be missing a great opportunity. Therefore, if your answer to their question automatically disqualifies you or them, find a way to have the discussion over the telephone so the both of you can find a way to make it work.

Negative (or 'NO') Reponses: Just like any objection, they come in different forms. You may get the simple, "Unsubscribe," or, "Not interested" messages, or the prospect could give more detail explaining the issue they have like, "We're under contract until the end of the year". So be aware that not every NO means no. Sometimes they just mean, "Not now". At the end of this book there's a great chapter on how to overcome objections, but for now the question is, what to do when we get negative or NO responses? The answer depends on how many leads you have versus how many you need. If you have a big potential market and your team is small, then you can target enough prospects that you don't have to even worry about the NOs you get. On the other hand, if you'd like to generate the highest volume of meetings or your market is small, and you need to convert the most leads possible, then I recommend picking up the phone and reaching out to the prospect.

Even though this person is starting with a NO, you're already at a higher advantage than if you were to call this person cold. They already know who you are, now they've heard of your company, and they know what the call is about. This is your starting point. You're going into the call with a mini-relationship that has been built. Many times, you even know what their issue is which gives you time to prepare for your response. These are luxuries that you do not get with cold calling. This is another reason we never want our first contact with a prospect to be a call.

Turn-Around Script for 'NO' Responses

This structure of this script is credited to sales and business consultant, Peter O'Donoghue of the U.K. Many know him for his online training course: *The Prospecting System*. What I like about the script is it comes off as if you've accepted the NO answer and your only goal is to see if you should EVER contact the prospect in the future. In practice, we ask three questions to identify a potential problem with their current situation, and then we offer to provide a solution to that problem in the form of a free product. That gift will be given to them in exchange for their time, in a future meeting. Let's jump in and we'll go deeper.

> **Prospector:** *Hi John, this is Michael with MindStorm. I was just about to reply to your email but thought it made more sense to give you a quick call. In your email, you mentioned that you aren't taking on any outside consultants at this time, and I just had 3 quick questions that will take less than 60 seconds to see if there would ever be a fit in the future. Is that okay?*

> **John:** *Okay, but I only have 60 seconds.*

> **Prospector:** *Of course. Do you have an inside sales team?*

> **John:** *Yes, I got 3 guys on the telephone who set appointments for 2 sales reps that are in the field.*

> **Prospector:** *How many meetings are they producing for your reps each week? (Ballpark.)*

> **John:** *Well this is a high-ticket item so if we can average one meeting a week per appointment setter then I'm happy.*

> **Prospector:** *And the third question, what do you think is your biggest challenge when it comes to generating high quality appointments for your sales reps?*

John: *We reach out to C-Level executives of large corporations and it's impossible to reach these people. It's not a volume business; it's about getting the right meeting set.*

Prospector: *You mentioned this is a challenge for you. How? (Digging deeper to find the pain).*

John: *Well if I had twice the leads we'd probably do 3x the business, so we're limited. And we've tried everything under the sun; nothing works in this industry except what we're doing. And we're doing it, but it's a lot slower than we' like.*

Prospector: *John, based on what you told me, you'd be a perfect fit for a strategy session with our CEO, George Athan. In that meeting, there will be three major benefits for you:*

1. *He will uncover hidden flaws in your current process that is killing potential opportunities*
2. *He'll show you a completely new way to land those hard to get meetings. This one strategy can generate 3x the number of leads you're getting each week.*
3. *He'll give you the exact process, scripts, and templates a similar company to yours used to generate an extra $1.5 Million dollars in business.*

We normally charge for trainings like this, but we'd love the opportunity to share these strategies complimentary, in an effort to introduce ourselves. Since these sessions get booked rather quickly, the first appointment I have open is _____. Would that day work for you?

The script here does a fantastic job of bribing the prospect to take the meeting. It offers so much value that it compels the prospect to say YES. You don't have to go crazy and offer the house. You can make it as simple as a strategy session, but it's how you describe the *strategy session* that's important. We want the prospect to see so much value in the meeting that they would *pay you* to get the information you are willing to provide at no cost.

The first two questions are simple, closed ended, qualifying questions. The prospect can easily answer them, feeling like he's two thirds the way through and almost done. The third question is meant to find his pain through an open-ended question. The answer to this question is what establishes the *need*, to get the meeting. If the prospect doesn't admit there is a problem, you have no justified reason to ask for a meeting because they will not find any value in the bribe. The bribe's value is that it offers a solution, and solutions are needed only when there are problems. My recommendation is that you go past three questions and keep digging deeper into that third question to really find the problem. You want to understand the pain, and maybe press on it a little more so your prospect sees the value in your solution. The better job you do at building leverage, the better the outcome. We'll go into a great process for that in section three, Sales Machine.

Chapter 8

The Speed Path

Throughout this book I've referred to a path that you lead your prospect through during their buying journey. Just like in real life, there are many routes one can take to reach a destination. Our goal is to create the shortest and smoothest route the prospect can take to reach the destination of making a purchase from you. I call this the Speed Path. It's not just a fast lane designed to speed right through the journey, but it's also the shortest route. It's designed to help the prospect get everything they need, to be comfortable with making the decision to buy from you, in the shortest amount of time. Anything outside of this path increases the time it takes to get the deal closed, and leaves money on the table. If you don't have a route like this established you can't possible offer any help in the buyer's journey. You would just have to hope that they find their own way.

If you fail to provide direction for the prospect, you risk them taking the long way, the more scenic route. This lengthens your sales cycle as you wait for them to take all those extra and unnecessary steps before they end up choosing you. Even worse, while they're taking the scenic route and visiting all of your other competitors, "just to see" what they have to offer, your prospect may end up taking direction from someone else along the way, ending up at a completely different destination. Hint: It's not buying from you! This is the importance of guiding your prospect through this process and having a path for them to follow. By knowing in advance what the Speed Path is, and establishing its boundaries, you can see when they're following the path perfectly and when they make a wrong turn.

To create a Speed Path, it's important to break up your sales process into very small steps. Expecting a client to take a big step will require them to make a large commitment on their end and take on more risk. At best, this will drastically slow your prospect down in moving along the path. At worst, if asking a prospect to take too big a step too early in the process, you risk losing them completely. Our strategy is simple, break up your process into as many small steps as possible so that no single step is too big or too scary. It's simply one small step. This will allow your prospect to run through them, getting to your destination faster. In the beginning, it may be at a crawl pace but with a few steps they may start walking, then taking bigger steps, then jogging, then running, and finally sprinting through the finish line. It's all about confidence. Confidence in you, your product, your company, and themselves, that they will be successful with your offering. Each step they take and each milestone they pass makes them that much more confident that this is the right decision and that they're moving in the right direction. As humans, we're driven to be consistent in all areas of our lives — our values, beliefs, the words we speak, our opinions, and actions. Once someone performs an act, a decision has been made and a stance has been taken on a subject. He or she strives to make future behavior match this past behavior.

It becomes increasingly hard to break this consistency as more commitments are made. Each step your prospect moves along the Speed Path makes it easier and more compelling to continue down that path. This reinforces a couple of things for us. First, if each step helps us, why would we want to have big steps in the process? We wouldn't because that would only mean we had fewer. We'd want to break each big step into many smaller ones so that each action your prospect takes increases the likelihood that they will continue down the path. Secondly, this also confirms the benefit of having a controlled path for your prospects to follow. Without proper direction, they can easily take an action that is not conducive to reaching the destination you hope for.

Say that your prospect has an initial conversation with you and then says, "Let me do some research and get back to you". A seasoned salesperson would make sure that there was a follow up meeting with a date and time set before that conversation ended. She or he also would send case studies, testimonials, white papers, and other marketing material so that the prospect had the right material to read when doing their 'research'. An inexperienced sales person might leave that call without knowing if they'll ever speak to the prospect again, or any idea what the prospect will be looking for to help with their decision. There's a lot of hoping in this scenario. What happens if the prospect's approach to research is having conversations with your competitors to compare you? They may engage in conversation with a more seasoned salesperson who then takes them down their own Speed Path. It only takes one action to change your client's direction, which is why it's so important to have a well thought-out path that guarantees the best experience for your buyer on their journey. A path that deters your prospects from getting lost, because one step out of bounds can easily become a slippery slope that leads to purchasing from your competitor!

Once you have such a process that stacks all the odds in your favor, follow that process with stubborn discipline. The probability of your sales process converting opportunities to sales is directly tied to the revenue you generate over time. Think of a casino's revenue, which is generated by the probability of the house's edge. In Blackjack, the casino has between a .5% to a 1% edge over people using basic strategy, depending on the version of the game. Many people try to follow 'the book' (basic strategy) but either don't fully know it or make emotional decisions. This means, the average player is actually playing at a 2% disadvantage to the house. Although a casino may lose on any one hand, they generate revenue by pumping as much money they can through that .5%-2% house edge. Odds of winning **X** the opportunity (in dollars) **X** # of transactions= revenue. This goes for both you and the casino.

The house edge in slots can be anywhere from 3%-17%. Do you see why there are more slot machines than blackjack tables? If you owned a casino, which would you rather more people play? Which is why if you have a process that has a 30% win-rate and another one that has only 10%, wouldn't you want to take everyone down the 30% path? Once you realize that this is nothing more than a math equation, your revenue will skyrocket.

Qualifying Calls

Once we get a positive response from our outreach efforts, we want to move them down the Speed Path. In some cases, we can move the prospect through multiple stages along the path within one conversation. This makes sense for sales that are easier in nature and completed within a few conversations. This stage should last on average 10 minutes. It's primarily to see that there is a need for your product and you're dealing with a person who has the authority to say YES. You're not talking about budgets (yet) and you aren't going too deep into their needs. You're definitely not talking about your offering. This is an opportunity to establish a relationship, build trust, and quickly qualify the prospect. If they're not your ideal client or they're not the person who can authorize the purchase, it's important that you discover this immediately. Taking someone with insufficient authority through the sales process is just bad practice. Not only is it a complete waste of your valuable time, but it makes it hard to go above that person's head once they've committed their time to engaging with you. They will butcher your sales presentation by taking your 30-minute demo and turning it into a 3-minute summary for their boss.

Discovery Meeting (Telephone or Face-to-Face)

The discovery process is designed to help you understand where your prospect is today, where they're looking to be tomorrow, and what challenges stand in their way of getting there. Being effective in the discovery process will show you what topics are most important, and exactly where you fit into the picture. This will set you up to give a great presentation because you'll be able to speak to the specific interests of your prospect. We'll go into depth on the discovery process as this is a big part of the overall sales process, but it's important to mention here because it's the next stage after the initial qualifying conversation. Again, you can move from qualifying to discovery on the same call but for more complex sales that require multiple engagements, there are many benefits to separating these conversations.

By separating these two calls, it makes your initial qualifying conversation more genuine because it shows that your only interest is to see if there is a need for your product or service. You're not trying to sell anything, you don't even know if he would be a good customer for you. You're just engaging in conversation to see if there is a mutual interest. This gives you power because it shows you're not desperate. It shows you're not so eager to make a sale that you'd take anyone and everyone. It shows that you are selecting clients; they're not just selecting you. Ideally, your prospector should not be your salesperson. This translates into: your prospector manages the responses and qualifies the prospect with the initial 10-minute qualifying call, and then passes the qualified lead to your salesperson, who does the discovery process. If you are the same person today, that's okay. Over time as you and your organization grow, it will benefit you to separate these responsibilities, making an assembly line for generating clients.

Smaller transactions or sales that don't involve big decisions being made can often benefit from a 'One Call Close' approach. This is where you can go through all sales stages in one sales call, whether that's over the phone or in person. This approach is very effective when it comes to sales that don't have much risk associated to going forward. An example of this can be a SaaS company with low cost subscriptions. If targeting small businesses, and there's not a large investment of money required and not much time associated to implementing the software after purchasing, then qualifying and discovery questions can usually be asked during a demo or presentation.

Let's start from the top and go through this so you always know where you are and understand what needs to happen next to quickly get to the goal of getting the new account or acquiring your new client.

Outreach: This is any effort you've made to initiate contact and bring both the problem and solution right to your ideal buyer. You've reached out multiple times, immediately demonstrating the value you bring, and making an offer they can't refuse.

Response: The prospect replies to you with either a positive, neutral, or negative response. They either, see the value and want to move forward, have been intrigued by your offer and have questions before they commit to moving forward, or don't find value and do not want to move forward. Our goal is the same for all three, to move this to a telephone call or a face-to-face meeting.

Bridge: This is your communication with the prospect, bridging their response to a sales call or meeting. The fact that they engaged with you is the reason the dialogue should continue to see if there is a fit between your company and theirs. Just because the prospect responded negatively, doesn't mean that the conversation should be over. This is your opportunity to bring new information to the table, offer even more value, and then again attempt to set a meeting. Some of your most lucrative opportunities will come from turning around responses that were initially negative.

Qualify: Before you can ask a prospect to invest time going through your sales process and before you invest any more time yourself, it's important to make sure that they qualify. In this stage, we need to establish:

- Do they have a need or desire? (a problem you solve or goal you can help achieve).
- Does this person have the authority to make the decision or move this forward?
- Does this prospect fit in your ideal client profile?

These questions are very important because if any of the answers are NO then this could not and should not move down the Speed Path. If this prospect doesn't fit your ideal client profile, then you're taking a risk that this would end badly, even if you get the sale. Only target those companies that you are the best for and they are the best for you. Everything else leads to slow growth. This last question may help you identify those who won't qualify financially just by asking questions about their business, without having to discuss budgets.

Transitioning to Discovery

Establish Need or Desire: In order for your prospect to want to move to the Discovery stage, they have to see that they have a problem you can solve or a goal that you can help them achieve. Without this there's no reason to go any further so make sure that you ask at least one qualifying question that establishes that they have interest in the benefit your product or service provides before trying to set the next meeting.

Using Rhetorical Questions: Rhetorical questions are good, because you already know the answer you will get, but be careful because it can come off very salesy. If I were to ask, "John do you want to grow your business?" that would just sound ridiculous or facile. Instead I might say, "John, on a scale from 1-10, how important is business growth this year for ABC Corp, with 10 being very important?"

Framing: Since we want highest possible number here, knowing in advance that you're going to ask a question like this gives you the opportunity to use a strategy called priming. If you use the word 'ten' a few times in the conversation before this question is asked, then 'ten' becomes an easy answer to give back to you. Research into persuasion techniques suggests that priming with higher numbers may influence the person to report higher numbers on your 1-10 scale. At the end of my question, my statement, "10 being very important," again uses the word '10' and then gave the prospect a value for it, which is very important. When asking rhetorical questions that you know are very important to the prospect, using this strategy often gets an easy '10' response.

Control the Message: It also helps to reconfirm that there is a need, using a statement. For example, if the response I get is 8 then I say, "Okay great, this is important to you". In fact, if I get a 6 or better I'm interpreting that meaning to be important and I confirm it in a statement. A six would get "Still important or somewhat important." They would have to correct me and say, "No it's not important at all."

Stay on the Speed Path: Make sure that you keep your conversation at a high level and never get into specifics about your product or service at the Qualifying or Discovery stage. Save that for the Presentation stage. If they try to take control and ask you to get into details, give them a high-level response and go back into qualifying or discovering. Use their desire to find out more as the carrot to keep this moving forward to the next stage. If you lay out all the information they want before you take them through this process in the correct sequence, then you'll take the magic out of your trick and it will lose both the mystique and the dramatic effect you're aiming for. You also risk the prospect making their decision prematurely. Without going through the emotional experience of feeling pain with the status quo during your discovery, and then progressing to feeling the pleasure of seeing a brighter future with your solution in place during your presentation, then you're risking that they make a decision without the very thing needed for the decision to go in your favor: emotions. Using the same analogy earlier of the Speed Path being a road traveled, these emotions provide the necessary fuel. Without this emotional fuel, your prospect can't move forward, and the deal will stall wherever they are on their buying journey.

You now have all the parts and the instruction manual to build a lead generation machine of your own. In the next section we will build your Sales Machine to turn your high value meetings into high value clients.

SECTION 3

SALES MACHINE

Chapter 9

Reframing Pain & Pleasure

If you change what your prospect associates pain and pleasure with, you can change their behavior.

The 'Pleasure Principle' is a term coined by Sigmund Freud meaning that, to satisfy biological and psychological needs, all human behavior is driven by two forces; our need to avoid pain and our desire to gain pleasure. This means that everything we do is for a reason. We never do random things, without a motive. This is a massive plus for those of us wanting to create a predictable system for acquiring clients. If we understand what our prospects associate pain and pleasure with when it comes to making a buying decision, then we can *predict* the outcome! Even better, if we can shape what prospects associate pain and pleasure with, then we can *shape* the outcome.

Many of the tools in this book have a powerful effect on people, so it's important to use them with absolute integrity. To quote Uncle Ben from Spider-Man, "With great power comes great responsibility". And just like any powerful tool that can be used for good or for bad, it's your responsibility to use these tools ethically. Now back to our show.

When we're making decisions we're always weighing the costs versus the benefits in every situation. If the benefits outweigh the cost, there's a net positive, and we decide to move forward.

On the other hand, if the cost is greater than the benefits, there's a net negative, and we don't. This is true when we're talking about your prospect's decision to go or not to go to the gym in the morning, and it's just as true when we're talking about their decision to purchase from you later that day.

When we talk about cost, that cost comes in many forms. Something can cost you time, opportunity, money, reputation. It can cost you emotionally, physically, etc. Any pain that might result from going forward is considered a cost. This also includes just the risk of loss, or even potential loss in the future. So, when your prospect is deciding on whether or not to move forward with your company, they're weighing the benefits they'll receive from your offering (*pleasure*) against the costs involved in going forward (*pain*).

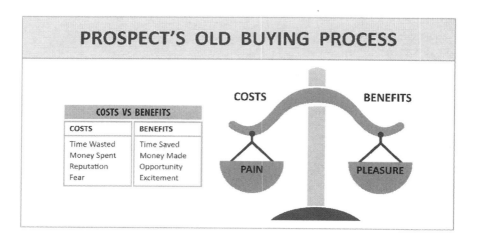

So, what's really happening is that it's not a cost vs benefit thing, it's really a pain vs pleasure thing. If the pain outweighs the pleasure and there's a net negative, they will say NO. But if the pleasure outweighs the pain, there's a net positive, they will say YES. What's significant about this is that when we talk about pain and pleasure, it's a *feeling*. This isn't a quantified cost vs benefit analysis that is done on a virtual spreadsheet in your brain using logic. This is a subjective, biased, often irrational decision being made on a purely emotional level.

If we know that we make buying decisions emotionally, and those emotional decisions are being made by weighing pain against pleasure, then imagine what can happen if we put pain and pleasure on the same side - we'd tip the scales!

How do we do that? Simple. Instead of having your prospect think about costs versus benefits in this emotional tug of war, let's have them think about the costs *plus* the benefits. What it would cost them by NOT having your solution in place and all the benefits of having them. It's like if both teams in that tug of war all pulled for one side, there would be no resistance.

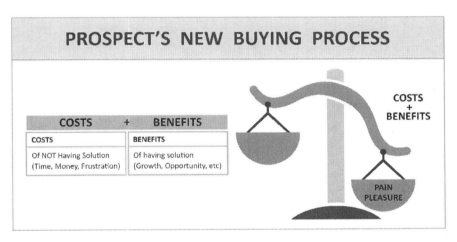

During our Discovery process, we're not just going to establish that there's a need, we're going to find out what it's costing the prospect to continue operating this way. What are the long-term ripple effects if they don't rectify this problem? What will it cost them financially, emotionally, etc. If the prospect is going to think about pain anyway, why not have them really consider the costs of not fixing these issues? This is something most buyers overlook. This happens because the salesperson failed to take control of the conversation or has the control but didn't take them down the Speed Path.

In Discovery, we're also going to find out the prospect's ideal outcome, so we can understand the exact benefits they'd like to experience if they were to design the perfect solution for themselves. This will give us insight into what's most important to the prospect, so we base our presentation on it and offer the most amount of pleasure possible.

Presenting becomes easy because the prospect already told us what they'd like to talk about and during this stage you offer exactly what they asked for, speaking on the specific benefits they are looking for. They literally tell you how to sell them. (Again, be ethical!). The rest of the presentation is just proving that you can deliver on that promise.

Go Fast and Far

When it comes to pain and pleasure the consensus is that we tend to take action faster in an effort to avoid pain than we would do to gain pleasure. This is most likely hardwired into us as a self-preservation mechanism where our instincts enable us to act fast in the presence of danger. In economics and decision theory, *Loss Aversion* refers to people's tendency to prefer avoiding losses to acquiring equal gains. As an example, imagine two scenarios where, Scenario A, you were about to become a victim of a theft, with $1,000 stolen from you, and, Scenario B, you were given the opportunity to make an additional $1,000. Most people will move faster reacting to Scenario A, preventing the $1,000 loss, than they would for the $1,000 gain in Scenario

B, even though the financial payoff is the same. Part of that is because in the first scenario that money is already ours and losing it would make us feel less than whole, where the money in Scenario B is a luxury. Losing that future money doesn't feel as painful as losing the present money. Remember, pain and pleasure are emotional responses based on perception, not based on quantifying and analyzing.

Some experts suggest that avoidance of pain is the greater motivator, causing us to take faster action and greater lengths to avoid it, than the efforts expended to gain pleasure. This is where I disagree. In my experience people will act faster to avoid pain, but only go far enough to where they are comfortable and/ or safe. But even when people take longer to act to gain pleasure, ultimately they go much further. It's the difference of *having* to do something and *wanting* to do it. If an employee is only working harder because they are at risk of losing their job, they will only work as hard as they must, not to get fired. Once they are out of the danger zone and the risk is gone, so is the motivation. If an employee is working harder because they want to make a name for themselves, they will work much harder for longer. They don't tend to stop at that first promotion. When people seek to gain pleasure, goals tend to be more ambitious and greater initiative is taken. Momentum builds, and each milestone creates the motivational fuel to reach the next milestone. Now let me show you how we use this information to build the client machine.

Sequence is Important: Pain then Pleasure

If pain makes you move fast and pleasure makes you move further for longer, we'd want to first use pain to get your prospect to want to act fast. Then, as they're on the move (in their mind going down the buying path) and momentum is building, we follow that up with pleasure to get them to go far. Have you've ever had an experience where you were procrastinating doing something that you knew you should do and then something happened that forced you to start the project? If you've experienced this, you know that once you start then you're on a roll. Once you get your prospect to decide in his or her mind that they are going to take care of a problem, then it's like, well if we're doing this then let's do X, build Y, and so on. They become excited about the future possibilities.

In the old mafia movies, the bad guys were great salespeople. They really knew how to motivate someone to do what they wanted. They used both pain and pleasure together. They said, "If you do this job I'll give you $100,000 and if you don't, I'll kill ya!" Ok, maybe that was a terrible example but that's the point! There aren't many examples out there, because usually people are only using one motivator or the other. In the upcoming chapters, you will learn the process that sells the way your prospects buy. They buy on emotion and justify their decision with logic. Using the two motivating forces that drive all human behavior, we will create pain to make the prospect feel as if they *have to* take action and then create pleasure to make them *want to* take action. Finally, we supplement those emotions with logic to validate that it's the right decision, showing them that they *should* take action. Green lights all the way.

Chapter 10

Connecting

Now that we've built a machine to consistently generate sales meetings on demand, it's time to learn how to develop those initial conversations into sales opportunities and then convert those sales opportunities into new clients. Before we move into the next phase of your process, it's important to talk about connecting with your prospect.

I learned everything I know about connecting from my good friend and business partner Felissa Hayes. Watching her with people is nothing short of amazing. She's one of those people that you can meet for the first time and feel like you just made a friend for life. But it's more than her being likeable. She creates the feeling of admiration, while her knowledge and delivery commands respect. How she is with people goes beyond rapport, and since she's by far the best I've ever seen at relationship building, I've tried to put as much of her magic into this chapter.

In psychology, it's long been acknowledged that as humans we have a fundamental need to connect with people and feel loved. Maslow calls this *Love and Belongingness* in his Hierarchy of Needs. Artur Manfred Max Neef labels these needs as *Affection and Participation* in his Human Scale Development, and Tony Robbins refers to this as *Love and Connection* in his Six Human Needs.

We create bonds and build relationships to meet these fundamental needs. In fact, they're so deep in our core that fulfilling these needs takes priority over others and it's more important to your prospect than the luxury of benefiting from your product or service. That's right, your solution to your prospect's problem is a luxury that can only be afforded after their basic human need of connection has been met.

Armed with this knowledge, you can now design a different approach to your prospecting, selling, and client servicing. The approach can be summed up with this rule: The relationship comes first, business comes after. By adopting this mindset, you can save yourself from amateur mistakes like moving too fast, skipping the relationship-building component and trying to sell too quickly. The moment the sale moves further than the relationship has developed, you will get resistance from your prospect because they'll feel things are moving too fast. And it's all about the feeling.

Obviously, this doesn't apply to transactional purchases like buying a cup of coffee, but this certainly applies when selling any product or service to someone you'd call a client. Remember we said that the definition of a client is 'one that is under the protection or patronage of another; a dependent?' Well how can they feel they can depend on you if you don't establish some sort of a relationship first? They can't. As a side note I will say that a large portion of the relationship can be established with the company or the brand. Large companies with huge marketing budgets can connect with the market through sheer persistent programming, and this star power can be enough. But for most companies, it's the salespeople that have the single biggest impact on the relationship with the buyer and how the buyer will perceive the company.

One day during a sales workshop, I was giving a training on this topic and was asked, "What's the appropriate amount of time

I should be connecting with prospects?" He was really asking how long he needed to do this 'rapport' thing before he could get down to business and start selling. His misconception was that connecting was a technique or an action to take, but connecting would better be defined as the process of building and leveraging the relationship. Connecting should be an ongoing effort, because building the relationship should be an ongoing effort. Relationships, just like everything else, are either growing or they are dying. That's true regardless of whether we're talking about business or personal relationships, and we should be making every effort to continue to grow every relationship we value.

The very process we're describing of generating clients is simply the process of cultivating and growing relationships, from prospect to client. Relationships can go far beyond that. These same people can be a referral partner, joint venture partner, business partner, friend, and even considered family over time. A transaction happens as a byproduct of a partnership that happens between two or more people. Just like any partnership, if you take those relationships for granted you are risking the partnership ending and the future transactions stopping. Therefore, connecting must be a constant and ongoing effort if you value that relationship.

Dangers of Rapport 'Techniques'

We've all heard how important it is for your prospect to know, like, and trust you but now it's time to understand why at a deeper level so that we connect more effectively and avoid the pitfalls that can come with trying to use a technique.

What we're talking about is one of the most basic fundamentals of persuasion, to connect with another human being on a level that they take in all of the information you are giving, without the underlying skeptic filtering mechanism trying to find some ulterior motive. Imagine if you had the ability to speak directly to someone's subconscious, what doors would that open for you?

When we're around people we completely trust, we're much more relaxed and less tense because we don't have our guard up. This is the point at which we are the most open to suggestion. The reason sales people struggle to effectively utilize rapport techniques is because their behavior is immediately recognized by the prospect on an unconscious level, and this triggers doubt. It raises a red flag that creates tension and has the prospect's guard up even more than if no technique was used. The very idea of using a technique to create a false illusion of connection is the *exact opposite* of rapport. By doing this you have just violated one of the core components of true rapport, TRUST.

This is important because the entire relationship hinges on only two factors, they trust you and you add value to that relationship. So, if you offer value but they cannot trust you, their survival instinct kicks in and they'll become fearful of engaging. This isn't a choice, this is a reaction. We've been hardwired to fear things we can't predict.

When we want a prospect to feel like they know, like, and trust us it's simply for the following reasons. 'Knowing us' gives them the *ability to determine* if they should trust us or not. If they don't know enough about us (or our company) then they feel like they can't make that determination. 'Liking us' says they've gotten enough information to determine that they can trust us. We tend to like people that have similar values, so when the prospect likes you, they feel that the admiration they have for you is a good indication that you can be trusted. The reality is that this isn't a good measure at all because it's just a feeling, but again, most decisions (if not all) are made emotionally and validated later through logic.

Trust

Trust is the most important topic of relationship building because things can only move as fast as the speed that trust is established. You can ask anything from the person who has complete trust in you. Think of at least one person in your life right now who trusts you completely and take a moment to imagine what response you'd get if you asked that person to borrow their car. What if they needed help marketing their business and you ran a digital marketing agency? Would it be a hard sell? Of course not. If they truly knew you could deliver the result they wanted, getting a YES would be immediate. There would be no, "Send me your references" or, "Let me think about it". You have what they need, you offered to help, the answer is YES! Trust shortens sales cycles and shorter sales cycles means more annual revenue because you are generating more sales in that same 12-month period.

So how do we build a stronger level of trust, faster? There are two forms of trust: Capability and Intention. The person you are trying to influence must believe that you are *capable* of delivering the result you promise. But it's much more than merely being competent, it's that you are the authority on the topic. That you know *more* than they do on that topic so that they can trust following your direction. This is the reason educating your customer is so important in sales.

Once you've shown your knowledge you demonstrate that you're *able* to lead them to a better place. But before they move forward, your prospect must believe that you are doing this for *their* benefit, not yours. Obviously, they understand that you are benefiting from the transaction because you are not doing this for charity and everyone likes win-win partnerships, but the prospect's win must be the main driver. This is where they must trust your intentions. If there is any doubt that you are not doing this with their best interest in mind, you will immediately lose trust, and most likely lose the sale.

So, looking back to rapport tricks like 'Matching & Mirroring' or 'Pacing & Leading', fake smiles, chit chat about the weather, and talking about fishing because you see a picture in their office where he was on a fishing boat, these will all kill your sale. It breaks trust immediately because it screams that you're not being genuine. It says I'm lying to you in a small way so that you can buy my stuff, which goes back to not being able to trust your intentions.

Take the Lead

We know that during the sales process there's one person driving, and you have the option to be in the driver's seat or a passenger who's just along for a ride. If you accept being a passenger, then you'll have no control over the outcome or what happens at each stage. The prospect will dictate the topics of conversation, which then impacts what they focus on, which in turn influences what they feel, and ultimately directs what they do. If we know the best way to deliver every piece of information they need, and we can deliver it in the perfect way, shaping the sound, making it music to their ears like a perfectly orchestrated symphony, why would we want to hand over the baton asking them to be the conductor? They have no experience in how your presentation should be delivered. They don't even have anywhere near the experience you do in a situation like this. You've sold your service many more times than they have ever purchased that type of service. *You* are the expert. Don't make this a terrible buying experience for them!

Giving them control not only ruins the buying experience for the prospect but also hurts your company and brand by not delivering the highest perceived value of your product every single time. Your brand is only worth what the market thinks of it. So, when the buyer dictates the conversation and only asks you questions that relate to specific components of your offering, you are risking limiting your presentation to points that don't fully demonstrate the power behind your offering. Every time you give one of these subpar presentations, you are doing both your prospect and company a disservice.

Not only does this affect your brand, but you would also be doing yourself and the company a disservice by depriving it of revenue that it would be benefiting from if you had not given up control. When the buyer calls all the shots it creates the illusion of power, especially since they already know they are the one with the money, so ultimately, they will decide your fate. This mindset restricts them of a vital ingredient that's needed to make a purchase: desire. Not only must there be a need, but there must be desire as well. Your prospect must *want* to buy. Think about when you want something, but you are not sure if it will be available to you. How does that feel? Do you want it more? Of course. That emotional cocktail of excitement of the offer mixed with the fear of missing out can get you into a frenzy and trigger you to act immediately. People want what they can't have or what's limited, scarce, and exclusive. We know that when you can't have something the more you want it, yet the easier it is to attain, the less appealing it becomes. Handing over all the control and authority to your prospect will often create a mini power trip, creating the exact opposite feeling and the interest for your offer will diminish rapidly.

Rules to Live by to be Liked and Trusted

To be Liked:

Rule #1: Like them first. You can't fake this, you must genuinely like them. Find something that you like and focus on it. (Personality, laugh, knowledge, something!) People like people who like them, and dislike those who dislike them.

Rule #2: Compliment what you like and explain what you like about it. The reason this is rule #2 is because if you don't follow rule #1 and don't like them but try to fake compliment, you will lose trust and things will go terribly wrong. By complimenting you are directly telling them you like them (or something about them).

Rule #3: Become genuinely interested in them. If you are interested, you are perceived as interesting. Even more, if you are fascinated, you become fascinating. Ask questions, get curious!

Rule #4: Speak to them as if you've known them for years. Most people are nervous meeting new people. Unless you do it often, people are not naturally comfortable with this process so make it comfortable for them by speaking to them as if you have known them forever. In turn they will relax and feel like they've known you forever. This can be game-changing for you if it becomes part of your regular approach, because it touches on all three categories: know, like, and trust.

Rule #5: SMILE. This creates immediate connection and an unconscious positive response. But be sure the smile is real because people can spot that as well. The difference between a real smile and fake one is in the eyes. Fake smiles are mouth only. This applies to the telephone as well. People feel it on the other end. Hence the phrase, "Smile and dial!"

Building Trust (Intentions):

Rule #1: First and foremost, only care about the benefit to your customer. If you add value to enough people's lives and put enough clients before your own self-interest, you will have more clients, and you'll have clients for life. Don't be short-sighted. This sounds obvious, but make it real because this isn't just a mission statement to look good on your website, this should be how you operate as a person.

Rule #2: Always speak to the benefit of the customer. Answer the WIIFM (What's in it for me?). By doing this, it shows that all your focus and all that you care about is your client benefiting. You'd be surprised how often salespeople say things like, "I'd love to see you get started" or, "I was hoping...". Your prospect doesn't care about what you were hoping for. They only care about what it means for them. The time that you have with your prospect is not infinite. This means that if your time with the prospect is limited, so are the number of words you can use. Don't waste them.

Rule #3: Make it abundantly clear that your only concern is their benefit. Many salespeople assume that the prospect should know this, and they fail to emphasize it with words. The prospect has dealt with many salespeople before you, who only cared about their own selfish needs and tried to push their product without demonstrating any concern for your prospect. Since he or she has been mistreated in the past, it becomes easy to assume all salespeople only want one thing. They need to be told that you will put their interest before yours. Explain to them that if it isn't a fit you would rather they get the right product from someone else and you'll even recommend where they should go. Show your integrity and do it genuinely. (I know I shouldn't have to keep saying the genuine part, but I promise you there are people right now skimming through this chapter to learn a new way of tricking a prospect into buying.)

Rule #4: Find out what's most important to them. Many things in life are preferences and we all have different values. You can be an expert on any topic, but you can't know what someone prefers. By asking and trying to understand their buying criteria, you demonstrate that you care about what's more important to them (not you). And showing is more powerful than telling. We'll talk about the buying criteria later but asking these questions demonstrates your willingness to provide what they are looking for.

Building Trust (Capability):

Rule #1: Become an expert. A real one. Learn your product better than everyone else. Understand your competitors' products better than their salespeople know them. Know your prospect's industry as well as they know them. (This is another benefit of picking a niche.) Spend time doing the research and become the expert on these topics because there is no faking this, you are either capable or you are not!

Rule #2: Educate the customer. Teach them what you know, and they will recognize your expertise immediately. Teach them how to compare, show them what to look for and how to buy. This is the fastest way for the world to see that you are capable; simply demonstrate it.

Rule #3: Be the authority. You must lead, not follow. In order for the prospect to take action based on your suggestion, you must take the lead and become the authority in that relationship. There is always a teacher-student, parent-child, employer-employee, doctor-patient relationship happening. During a sales conversation, you must be the authority and *make* recommendations so that they can be the person that *takes* the recommendations. Start small with things like, "Please sit here" or, "Grab a pen". Every suggestion they take makes it easier and easier to take the next, bigger, suggestion. Lead, not follow.

Rule #4: Show how others have benefited from following your lead. Tell success stories, give examples, show testimonials, case studies, etc. Nobody wants to be the guinea pig. Let them see social proof that you already have a following and these people's lives and businesses are better because of you.

Connecting in Action

By respecting the rule of putting the relationship before business, you will always know what to do in any given situation. If you truly care about your prospect, their needs, their business, and helping them become successful, then you won't need to be reminded to tell a prospect when it's not a right fit even though you don't want to turn down the business. You'll instinctively know to have a regular conversation first before talking about business. These things will be automatic because you'd have genuine interest in them and their story.

You'll often hear people say things like, "We're on the same page" or, "We see eye to eye" and these phrases describe what it's like to have a good rapport with someone. Things move easy from that point and sales can move fast. Compare that to the opposite of rapport when you don't like who someone is as a person, and you don't trust a word they say. That sale isn't happening. It's easy to see the point when we talk extremes, but the reality is that most salesperson/prospect interactions fall somewhere in the middle of those two extremes. So, the prospect doesn't hate the salesperson, but doesn't love him/her either. Which means, after everything the salesperson says, the prospect must stop and ask himself, is that true? Does this really apply to my situation? Gas. Brake. Gas. Brake.

Put yourself in the buyer's shoes. When you really know someone, really like who they are as a person, and completely trust them, the buying process will move insanely fast. Magic happens because things are flowing. You can move from stage to stage down the Speed Path and you can make a buying decision pretty quickly. If we were to create a scale from 1-10, this scenario would be a 10. And on the opposite end of the spectrum, a 1 would be a person that you didn't know, you didn't like, and didn't trust at all. So, what happens when you're connecting with a prospect at a 5? You get objections like, "I want to think about it" or, "I want to talk it over with others", or, "Send me some references".

This is a person who has said they have a problem that needs to be solved, they liked what you offered, but they still don't know that they want to move forward. They haven't given you a NO because it is a good fit, but they just aren't 100% confident it's the right choice, so they ask for more time. When the objection is that they want to ask someone else, that instantly tells you that someone else's opinion or recommendation holds more weight than yours. Because if they had 100% confidence in your product, your company, your expertise, and your intentions then your recommendation would be all they needed. They wouldn't second guess your professional opinion.

When they ask for references, that says I need to verify that what you're saying is true. There's nothing wrong with verifying and it's a good practice with every major decision, but the point is that it's also very logical. Logic showing up in a sales conversation that is designed to be emotional can be telling. It's either that they weren't taken down the emotional process we'll discuss in the next chapter, or if they were taken down that process then there's maybe a small trust issue. When people get too excited too fast and move down the buying process further than trust has been established, they feel that little shot of fear which acts as a warning to slow things down a bit.

By understanding how this works, we can methodically construct how our conversations should play out in advance and deliver everything the prospect will need to feel comfortable, with precision timing. The benefit to building a Client Machine is that you will never have to sell off the cuff again, randomly poking around in the dark, hoping you happen to say the right things. There's another benefit to understanding how this works. It will come in handy when you get objections like those mentioned before because once you understand the root issue, you can do more than just have a jazzy rebuttal to respond with. You can give them what they actually need to move forward: confidence in their decision.

The Most Interesting Topic in the World – THEM

People like to talk about themselves and things that they are interested in. So much so that it's to a fault. When I watch interactions between people it amazes me because it's almost like they're just waiting for the person speaking to finish so they can talk about themselves. And when that person is speaking, the other person is politely smiling and giving the uh-huh, just so they can fake being interested just long enough for that person to stop talking so they get their turn, and the cycle continues!

Often, people are just talking at each other and not to each other. This doesn't make someone a bad person, it's just that they have way more interest in the things in their own world than the things in that other person's world. This happens most when people have very little in common, and is the polar opposite of rapport. The more we have in common with someone, similar values and beliefs, the more we tend to like them. So, if our goal is to build a relationship with the prospect, then the best strategy would be to allow them to talk about things they are passionate about and find common ground. If it's topics that you are not familiar with then it's a great opportunity to ask questions and learn more. Again, if you are truly interested in this person than any of their experiences will be interesting to you.

We're naturally wired to be the center of our own universe and this is another survival instinct. We're constantly taking in information from the world around us and filtering that information to determine how each of those things will affect us personally. Every piece information we take in, we're attaching a meaning to, so we can interpret it as 'good' or 'bad'. We label these good or bad depending on whether they will help us or hurt us in our game of life. I'm not suggesting that humans are all self-centered, in the traditional personality sense. The most selfless human being attempts to win their game of life by helping as many people as possible. They too, are at the center of their universe and take in information to determine if it can help them help others. We instinctively come first, then others. If you have any doubt, just ask anyone to look at a picture that they're in with others and ask them who is the first person they looked at. How did they determine if they liked the picture or not? Usually it's based on how they felt they looked in it.

So, what the hell does this have to do with getting clients? A lot actually. This is where the *What's in It For Me* (WIIFM) question comes into play. If we understand how our prospects are absorbing information and what they will do with it, then we can do a better job of giving them what they need to build a stronger relationship.

> **Side note:** We've moved from giving them what they need to go to the next stage in the sale, to now giving them what they need to go to the next stage of the relationship. Progress is happening. Okay so we've established that people like to talk about themselves and their interests because, well... it's more interesting! (This includes you and me as well, obviously.) We also know that as we take in information there are two questions we're constantly asking unconsciously: How can this hurt me? And how can this help me? (Most likely in that order.) All other information is filler. What do we do with these pieces of information?

In an effort to build a relationship, we want to add value to that person, any way we can. We want them to have an amazing experience engaging with us, which in turn, will have them want to engage more often and for longer periods of time. To accomplish this, we make sure that we never fight for attention like everyone else. When they stop talking we're not eager to jump in and talk about ourselves. Instead, we have more questions, so they can go deeper into the topic. We compliment them when the opportunity arises. We make statements that reinforce their own beliefs. We become fascinated and they can feel it.

Let's be clear, I'm not recommending that you act like a star struck fan. It's important that you maintain a higher status than your prospect or at the very least, you're on the same level. If you become a supplicant, not only will you lose any chance of getting a sale, but you wouldn't even be building the relationship. If they don't respect you then you wouldn't be of value to them and everything goes downhill. Your goal is to hold the highest status possible in that relationship and still express a lot of interest in them. This combination in sales is powerful because it says, I don't need you, but I want you. Or in business sense, I don't need your business, but I do want it. The best part is that it says all that without saying anything. Demonstrations are far more powerful than declarations.

Conversation Starters and Relationship Builders

At different stages of the relationship, your conversations will change. The more you know about someone the more you can *talk* about, and the less you know about someone the more you can *ask* about.

Here are some conversation openers to play around with, where you can substitute words to fit your prospect:

- *How long have you been at ABC Corp?*
- *Have you spent a big part of your career in the hospitality industry?*
- *What made you get into the consulting business?*
- *Your restaurant is amazing. I've never seen a kitchen kept so spotless. How do you do it?*
- *I was reading an interesting article you wrote on.... (Give compliment... Ask question)*
- *I noticed on your LinkedIn profile you... (Ask question)*

You don't need to read a book on how to ask questions, but it will benefit you to have a few 'go-to' questions so you can get the conversation started and keep it flowing. When people don't have conversation starters they resort to the most overused and abused topic in the world- the weather. Please don't talk about the weather, nobody is interested in it unless we're talking about something like a hurricane or other Acts of God. When salespeople don't have enough questions to start a conversation and they don't go the weather route, they usually end up making statements about themselves to start conversation. But when you do that without knowing anything about the person you're talking to, you risk touching on topics that your prospect has no interest in or can't relate to, or worse, offend them.

Recently I was listening to a recorded sales call that demonstrated this perfectly. I was listening to the recording to critique it and use the feedback as a training session for a client's sales team. The salesperson started off by talking to the prospect with great energy in a tone that came off as if the two had known each other for years.

Salesperson: *Hi Peter, this is John from XYZ*

Prospect: *Hey John, right on time.*

Salesperson: *Yes, I try to be. Hey, did you catch that Ranger game last night?*

Prospect: *No, I don't really follow sports. Who has the time?!* (Apparently John did. That slacker!)

Salesperson: *Oh man, it was amazing. They were tied 3-3 and lost in overtime!* (Didn't this guy just tell you that he doesn't care?)

Prospect: *Oh yeah? (The interest is just oozing out of his voice.)*

Salesperson: *Yeah, I got to watch it with my son. It sucked that they lost but it was great to spend the time with him. Those are the moments you live for. I can't wait to take him to his first game. Do you have kids?* (John probably should have asked this question before he told Peter that the only purpose to life is spending time with children Peter never had.)

Prospect: *No, no I don't. But hey, I have a hard stop at 3:15pm. I'm sorry to have to cut this short today. Out of curiosity, what are the typical costs involved in this?*

You know exactly how that ended. Talking price before going through the process will almost never result in a sale. The prospect went straight to price because he was cutting the conversation short. And he only cut it short because the salesperson instantly broke rapport by showing the prospect examples of how their worlds and views are very far apart. Now, could they have 100 other things in common? Absolutely. But Peter will never know, because he probably won't have another sales conversation with John. The worst part about this call was that Peter initially responded well to John. He sounded happy that John called exactly 3pm on the dot and even acknowledged it, which means punctuality was important to him. John being professional, making it a point to call exactly at 3pm, so also values punctuality. This could have been the first thing they connected with. They could have bonded by talking about the pet peeve of salespeople calling 5 minutes late keeping you waiting. Instead John assumed that Peter loved sports, assumed he loved hockey specifically, assumed he had kids, and assumed that Peter shared that same belief that you live for the moments of watching sports with your kids. Remember the saying, don't assume, you make an **ass** out of yo**u** and **me**.

When is it Too Personal?

The stronger your relationship, the more personal you can get. The reverse of that is true too where the more personal you get, the stronger your relationship builds. Although it's true, be careful with that last statement. When they share something personal with you, they feel closer to you because it's the *act of sharing* something personal with you that brings you closer, not you invading their privacy asking personal questions. So, if they initiate it, that's fine. Share something personal back. If you initiate personal talk, then make sure that you share something first and ease into the questions.

We said earlier that if a conversation moves too fast towards a sale it creates that warning to slow things down. Similarly, a conversation getting too personal faster than trust is built will do the same. With that being said, there are immense benefits to getting a person to open up to you and you reciprocating with sharing things on that level as well. You build a ton of trust. They will now *know* you, *like* you, and *trust* you. Just make sure that you transition into this territory slowly because nobody wants to hear you complain about your spouse when all they wanted was pricing on a new copy machine!

Final Piece on Connecting

This subject was intentionally placed in this section of the book because we moved from lead generation to dissecting the sales process. Connecting with the prospect is always important, but it's absolutely vital here. Connecting means *relating* and that should happen during every single item of communication. If you send a prospecting email, letter, or message on social media that they can't relate to then you won't generate interest.

People build relationships with brands just by being receptive to messaging that they can relate to because that message offers value in some way.

Connecting is vital during the sales process because it allows each component of this methodology to build on the next. Steps are performed in a specific sequence which makes it extremely effective. If a deep level of trust is not established before attempting to go into the discovery questions, then the prospect will never open up to you. In fact, the opposite effect will happen. They'll resist going down the Speed Path with you. And if that happens, you will not create the emotional cocktail that makes them want to buy so intently. That's the magic behind the system. Attempting to go into discovery without connecting, is like asking a complete stranger intimate questions about their love life. You won't like the response you'd get to those questions.

Chapter 11

Discovering

Each component of the Client Machine is potent, but the Discovery process is by far the most powerful. When it's combined with all the other components in this book, the effects compound and your sales will increase exponentially.

This process was built with the end in mind (the prospect making a purchase) and then we reverse-engineered the steps. Your prospect buying is simply an action and just like every action, those are controlled or influenced by how we feel in the moments those actions are taken. If we can influence how they *feel*, then we can influence their action. We also know that how they feel is determined by what they are focusing on and thinking about. So, if we had a way to control what they're *focusing on* and direct what they're *thinking about*, then we can trigger the emotions that are most conducive to your prospect buying from you. So, how do we control what they're focusing on? Questions. Questions are the answer. They're the answer to a better sales process, a better buying experience for your prospects, and many more clients for you.

Obviously, everyone has their own version of the discovery process, whether you call it data gathering, needs assessment, or any other fancy name. That's nothing new. When the consultative sales approach was born, the approach was to have the prospect share information with the salesperson as if they were a consultant there to help solve the prospect's problems, hence the name.

In my opinion, a better analogy to the selling style would be a doctor's process: asking questions, reviewing symptoms, and maybe running some tests to diagnose the patient's condition. This is all done prior to recommending treatment. This is a great selling model in the B2B world which is why we've used it as the foundation of our methodology and built on that foundation to make it much more effective.

How did we do that? Well, just like a doctor, we ask questions to find out what caused the pain and where it hurts. And right before we offer to treat the wound, we squeeze that wound as hard as possible to create a very motivated patient. 😏

Motive and the Means

If someone doesn't have both the motive and the means to do it, they're not doing it. It makes no difference what we're talking about, you can apply that statement to any topic you'd like, and it will always hold true. One of your goals in the discovery process is to do a deeper level of qualifying. By the end of the discovery process we must establish that they have both the motive and the means to purchase from you.

To accomplish this there are 5 criteria that must be met:

1. Need
2. Desire
3. Validation
4. Justification
5. Means/Resources

Need: A need must be established. It's not enough for you to think they have a need, if *they* don't feel that they have one then they will not buy. If you see an obvious need then it's your job to help them realize it. The easiest way to establish a need is either to find pain or discuss a goal that they have and the need can be found in the gap between where they are now and where they want to be. More on that later.

Desire: Having to do something only takes you so far. But when you *want* something, the checkbook opens. One time I fell in love with a Breitling watch and, at $10k, it didn't tell better time than a $100 watch. In fact, I didn't need to wear a watch at all because every single device, including a phone that's always on me, shows the time. But I *wanted* it, so I bought it.

That same watch was stolen from my home and when that happened, I felt like I *needed* it because I was accustomed to having it. Insurance wouldn't cover it because I didn't have it listed on my homeowner's policy, so purchasing another one meant investing a total of $20,000 just to find out the time that I already had. And still that was an easy decision to make because I felt like I had to have it. The lesson here is that when you *need* something AND *want* something – the sky's the limit.

Validation: The next criteria that must be met is that your prospect needs to validate the truth in what you're saying. They would like proof or evidence of competence so that they can be confident you can deliver on your promise. There are three things being sold during the sales process; you, your company, and your product or service. Have validation tools for all three readily available so that they can be included in your presentation. By validation tools I mean case studies, testimonials, references, metrics, and so on.

Justification: To avoid your prospect feeling buyer's remorse, or cancelling on you at the very end, they must justify the purchase. My justification for the watches was that I worked hard, and it was a little reward for doing so. I use that example to show you that when you want something enough you don't even need a good reason to justify it, but we must have something to tell ourselves and others. The better the justification, the faster the sale. This is especially important if buying your product or service will require major changes in the prospect's organization. Whether they'll have to do things differently or lines of business will be affected in some way, they must be able to justify making these changes.

Means: Without the means, nothing is happening. The prospect must have the authority to make the decision, the funds to make the purchase, and logistical support or resources to ensure that working with your company will be a success. This includes capacity, personnel, technology, etc.

> **Side Note:** When it comes to authority, it's important to identify all the people that will have to sign off on this decision. Just asking if they are the decision maker will often get an incomplete answer. You might get a "YES" response because they may be a key person in making the purchase, but they may leave out the part that they still need others to agree on the decision. If this happens you'll end up relying on this person to communicate your message to their colleagues, completely butchering your sales presentation. It will be much more effective getting those people involved in the sales conversation earlier so that you can deliver your presentation to everyone.

Finding out who's involved in the decision should be established during the qualifying stage. There are risks in asking this too late.

Early in the sales process it's just a light question that doesn't feel like pressure or commitment, asking this question too late in the sales conversation can make a decision-maker feel as they should lie to you, so they can give themselves a way out. We want to preemptively eliminate all possible objections and one of those objections is they need to speak to their partner, boss, board, etc. One of my favorite ways to ask this question is, *"Assuming this is a good fit and assuming that we want to work together, who else would have to sign off for us to move forward?"* Asked this way, it does not make a non-decision-maker feel insignificant, so it doesn't trigger the need to lie to you, and it also aligns you and the prospect.

Set the Tone

After the first couple of minutes connecting, you are ready to get down to business. This is the moment where you want to set the tone and take control of the conversation. In Discovery, you'll be asking a lot of questions and if you're doing it right it will eventually start getting personal. To do this effectively it's important to mentally prepare the prospect for this so they know ahead of time what to expect. There's nothing worse than a salesperson asking question after question while you're wondering when it's going to end. If you've ever experienced this, the reason this feels terrible is because in your mind you were expecting to have a conversation. But that's not what we're having. We are going through a process to determine what their needs are so you can speak to the things that matter, and nothing else. This is for the prospect's benefit and if they know that in advance, they are completely fine with it.

Here is an example: *"Bob, we have many different services here at MindStorm, but I want to focus on the things that will have the most impact for you. So, in an effort to respect your time, we have a great process for determining what core services would benefit you most. I'll start by asking you some questions about your business and then I can talk to you about the things that are most important to you. Would that be okay?"* Then start your Discovery.

The power behind this process is that it will do just that. It will tell you what to talk to them about. Why would you talk about anything that wasn't important to them? Why would you think they'd want to hear you talk about anything other than what's most important to them? That's how ineffective old school 'pitches' are designed, to talk about what the salesperson or company think is important. Our process asks the prospect what they want to hear in the Discovery stage and gives it to them in the Presenting stage. Selling becomes very easy when a prospect tells you how to sell them!

Take Control

By setting the agenda for that meeting you are also taking control. You are driving the conversation, going down the Speed Path, and they are a passenger enjoying the ride. The person asking the questions has control of the conversation. And because of that fact, it's important to be prepared for the moment that your prospect has questions for you, so that you can regain control of your process. Otherwise a simple question can lead to a series of events that can destroy the chances of you and that individual doing business.

When someone asks you a question during this process you answer them directly, then immediately follow up with a question to take over the questioning. In this case it's best to ask a question that has something to do with the answer you just provided or their question so that it feels natural. Otherwise you can trigger an unnecessary power struggle with your prospect. For example, if they were to ask, "What are your response times?" You would answer, "Our response times are among the fastest in the industry, 30 minutes. Have you had a situation in the past where response was an issue?"

As you go higher up in the food chain of an organization and the larger the organization, you can expect to deal with many strong-minded individuals. Some people feel uncomfortable if they're not in control and as a fellow control-freak, I can tell you that we will do everything possible to dominate the conversation and dictate the terms. There are a couple of reasons why people do this and if you understand why they're doing it then you will know how to handle them in a way that works for everyone. I'd like to put our Discovery call on pause for a moment and review some core personalities.

The Rainmaker: This person is perfectly described in Oren Klaff's *Pitch Anything*. When discussing the 'power frame', he describes this coming from an individual with a massive ego. Their power is rooted in their status – a status derived from the fact that others give this person honor and respect. Imagine the CEO of a company with thousands of employees. Everyone around them follows their orders and they have the final say all the time. Salespeople are falling all over themselves, dying for the Rainmaker's business. Outside of work they are a person of high standing in social circles and are treated special everywhere they go. People are fighting for the Rainmaker's attention and affection, and the worst thing you can possibly do is fall into the category that every one of these people fit into.

The Rainmaker doesn't want to do business with a person like that. Will they do business with them? Possibly, if the offer was compelling enough but do they *want* to? No. What we're talking about is creating desire. Who the Rainmaker wants to do business with is someone that can lead them for once. It's refreshing when they find someone who is willing to take control and show them the way. Remember, they're coming to you because you're the expert in your specific line of work. If they know more than you about the problem you solve then they wouldn't need you because you wouldn't be able to help them. Which means, even if you know more but make them *feel* like they know more than you because you acted inferior, they won't do business with you because they won't trust your competence. How you demonstrate your leadership will determine what bucket they put you in, in their mind. This is an example where defiance can continue to build rapport, trust, and respect, while compliance can destroy it.

They key here isn't to try to aggressively dominate, that will only create a power struggle and they will become closed-minded to anything you say. You want to speak with a level of mutual respect, as if you are just as high in the food chain and this is your equal. Next you want to ask the Rainmaker to take small actions. Every time they comply, it makes it easier to follow your direction and take your next suggestion. Saying things like, "Jot this down" or, "Click on the link I sent you," starts to put you in a different light because they are usually the one giving the instruction. These subtle orders unconsciously place you as the authority in this conversation. Obviously, once you have achieved that position, it's on you to maintain that position. If you don't deliver and prove that you should be in control, you will lose it rapidly.

The Rain-Faker: Just like cockiness is a pretend confidence, the Rain-Faker is a pretend Rainmaker. This individual wants to be the Rainmaker badly, but he's not. He pretends by projecting an image of authority. The problem is that the more he has to pretend, the more he amplifies this persona to compensate.

Their insecurity creates a deep-seated need to show everyone they're boss. These are people who are spending money they don't have to create an image that's not real, to impress people they don't know. Initially it may be hard to differentiate them from Rainmakers, but it becomes clear the more you speak with them. These fake rainmakers have no problem being rude, or even insulting, to dominate you and the conversation, in order to sell who they are.

Therefore, Rain-Fakers are the exception to the rule of taking control. They are too sensitive to allow you to ever have control because in their mind if they don't dominate they are insignificant. That feeling of insignificance would create more pain inside them than you can ever create with your Discovery process and that pain would never turn into a sale.

The way to handle the Rain-Faker is by using the opposite strategy than you would for the Rainmaker. In this case it pays to be the subordinate. Allowing the Rain-Faker to feel as if they're in control but guiding their actions using weakness as your strength. The challenge with Rain-Fakers is that you can't press too hard on the pain because they're too sensitive and won't be able to take it. The upside is that asking any question that identifies pain will have a strong effect internally, even if they won't open up to you. If I ask you what's 2 + 2, you don't have to answer me, but you already did the math in your head. The same is true if you were to ask, "What happens if this problem doesn't get resolved?" They don't have to answer you to feel it.

The Control Freak: This is someone who tries to control everything, including your sales process. To their defense, it's also their buying process so they will do anything they can to control anything that involves them, especially if we're talking about something that involves money or risk. The Control Freak does this for one simple reason, they believe that they do things right (or better). They don't have much confidence in others and have a hard time delegating due to their fear that if they leave it in someone else's hands, things might go wrong.

The key to dealing with a Control Freak is to give them confidence in you. Immediately and often remind them that you are capable, to ease their fear. Not only speak it but demonstrate it with your actions. What's great about dealing with a Control Freak is that once they see that you can deliver, things shift immediately. There's no greater feeling for a Control Freak than to deal with competent people who are willing to take a load off of their shoulders. It may take a little time in the beginning, but once you prove yourself the Control Freak will follow your lead.

The Tire Kicker: This is the person who loves the process of buying but never buys. They're all about the journey, not the destination. So much so that if they were to get to the destination, that only means the journey is over, so they will avoid pulling the trigger at all costs. Their love of window shopping can fool you because they seem so interested in you, your product, and your company. They're giving buying signal after buying signal, but these are just false signals. The tire kicker is only included in here because their love of information can have them asking you a ton of questions and with questions come control of the conversation. You want to identify Tire Kickers fast and ask them direct questions in your Discovery that you would not normally ask so early if they were legitimate buyers. You can ask Tire Kickers questions like: What is your timeframe? or, When are you looking to get started? or, If you absolutely loved what I show you, are you ready to get started today?

If you see the signs, then qualify hard. There's nothing more expensive than people who waste your time. Obviously, you don't want to be rude and you want people to love your brand, just not at the expense of it. A good practice is to have webinars (live or on-demand) where you can speak to 500 of those people at once and it only costs you an hour of your time. As soon as you recognize a Tire Kicker or someone on the borderline of being qualified, you can direct them to the webinar. This way they can still get the information they want and hear the full pitch, while you spend that precious selling time with legitimate buyers, closing deals.

The Director: The name comes from Dr. Tony Allesandra's work where he divides behavioral preferences into four basic styles. Taken from Dr. Allesandra's website, here is how he describes the Director: *"Directors are driven by two governing needs: to control and achieve. Directors are goal-oriented go-getters who are most comfortable when they're in charge of people and situations. They want to accomplish many things now, so they focus on no-nonsense approaches to bottom-line results. Directors seek expedience, take authority, and plunge head first into solving problems. They are fast-paced, task-oriented, and work quickly and impressively by themselves, which means they become annoyed with delays. Directors are driven and dominating, which can make them stubborn, impatient, and insensitive to others."*

Directors aren't on a power trip, they're just used to taking charge. Also, they're not there for the chit-chat. They want to go in, get the job done, and get out so they can move on to the next thing. In sales, when you are dealing with a Director, you must deliver the information to them in a way they can pay attention to: short and to the point. When a Director is taking control and asking you questions, that's a good indicator that you are talking about things that are not relevant to them. This makes them ask pointed questions because they just want the bottom line. The challenge for you is that the 'bottom line' has no emotional value and bypasses their ability to feel the experience you want to deliver. If you allow the Director to take control, they'll squeeze all the data out of you and make a decision strictly analytical. We don't mind the prospect using logic in deciding, but we do mind them doing so prematurely. An analytical decision is a very slow decision and can easily stall the movement. Our goal is for them to make a series of small decisions of wanting to buy on emotion first and validate that decision (or justify it) using logic, after. In fact, we have a specific order of emotion we want them to experience. From the mind of the prospect, it goes like this:

Decision Process #1: Emotion – Move Away from Pain: *"My current situation is a problem and it's causing me pain. **I have to** do something about it. That doesn't necessarily mean I have to buy from you, but I do need to solve this problem."* This pain is created in Discovery and gets the prospect to start moving towards finding a solution.

Decision Process #2: Emotion – Move Towards Pleasure: *"I see a compelling future in your offer. It's exciting and **I want** that big promise your solution will give me. I want it now!"* This pleasure is created in the Presentation part of your sales conversation and creates a burning desire in your prospect.

Decision Process #3: Logic – Validation: *"I'm excited about this but I might be a little too excited. Hold on, I need to check. Is this thing real?"* The entire sales process done effectively will create a cocktail of emotions that are like rocket fuel to your prospect's buying journey. But we're wired to catch ourselves when we get too excited and the sale accelerates faster than the relationship is established, or faster than the trust in that relationship. This is in the Presentation part of your sales conversation. You must prove to them that everything you said is real and they have good reason to be excited.

Decision Process #4: Logic – Justification: *"I decided to buy, and I hope I made the right decision. I'm looking for reasons why this was the right thing to do. These are things that I can tell myself and when I tell others, they will agree it was the right move to make."* Helping your new client justify the purchase they just made is to be done after they commit to buying. It's important to note that this is to be used to solidify the sale, not to make it. People don't buy because it was the right thing to do, they buy because they want to. Showing them that it was the responsible thing to do then locks in that decision.

Now back to our Discovery....

Cementing your Role

As the relationship is forming we must be careful that we don't apply too much pressure too early in the conversation. Just like allowing time for the concrete to dry so the foundation is rock solid, we start with easy questions so that your prospect gets used to each of your roles in this relationship. You're the one with the authority asking the questions, and they follow your direction by answering. If we were to ask about their challenges too soon, we risk breaking rapport and making the prospect uncomfortable. If this happens, they'll take back control and won't continue with the roles you set because they can't trust you in that position. They learn that allowing you to have control will lead to you making them feel uncomfortable. Going forward they'll continue the conversation but only on their terms, which is them asking you for the information they want.

Even if it didn't go that far and they still allowed you to ask the questions, it's unlikely you'd get any real answers. Imagine talking to a stranger for just five minutes and they then ask you to share your most personal problems. Would you? Absolutely not. You'd tell them that everything was wonderful, which is the exact opposite of what we're trying to accomplish in Discovery. The same happens the other way around. Imagine you met someone and after five minutes they started telling *you* their most personal problems. How would that make you feel? You'd walk away thinking they're crazy, because normal people don't overshare. We have an inner gauge that tells us what information is appropriate to share, with whom, and when. The process in this book is designed to move the conversation in a sequence where the answer they give at each step transitions the conversation to the next, so it feels natural and never feels intrusive.

Understanding their World

Start with easy questions designed to get easy answers - answers that don't require much thought. Remember, it's not only about not being intrusive, you want them to feel as if it's easy to talk to you. Asking general questions that don't require much brain power do just that. Think about the questions that are important to understanding how their business operates. For me, I'd like to know about the types of customers they serve, how they get them now, what a customer typically spends buying their products, etc. For you, it will be different. The purpose here is to understand their current set up so you can start getting ideas where your expertise can be valuable to that relationship. We know that we'll get to ask them about their pain points but what we're doing is preparing in case the prospect feels they don't have any challenges to discuss. If that were to happen, and the prospect truly felt that they have no pain, there would be no urgent need to make any changes. But when we understand their world, it gives us the opportunity to show them the problems they are actually having but cannot see. We can educate them in a way that points to problems they weren't aware they had.

Every question I'm asking has a purpose. Just like a chess game, we don't waste any moves. We don't move pieces for the hell of it because that would be a waste of a turn. The same with your questions. We know that there's a finite number of questions they'll answer. We may not know in advance what that number is, but we do know that it's not unlimited, so we start with the ones that are most conducive to closing the deal. We also know there's a finite amount of time the prospect will give us, and we want to spend as much of that time on the topic of conversation that will lead to a sale: pain. (At least in Discovery).

In my business, the reason I ask about their ideal customers is because I can go back to all the different times I've helped previous clients target similar customers and refer to those successes when it's time. Those case studies will be used in my presentation as proof that we can help them get more. Also, by knowing the customers they target, I can also refer to the pain those clients experienced before hiring MindStorm. This way, in the event this prospect tells me he has no pain, I can bring up challenges others had when they targeted similar customers and see if the prospect can relate to any of that pain. This often jogs their memory quickly.

The point is that every question is strategic. Each question and its answer is giving me more information that I can use further down the line in my Discovery, Presentation, or Overcoming stage when handling objections. When I ask what a new client would be worth financially to a prospect, I'm asking so that it becomes easy for us to see if it makes sense doing business together or not. Once I know it makes sense, I can later use that information if the prospect has an objection related to cost. For example, let's say getting a new big account can generate $100,000 a year in business for you, why wouldn't you spend $80,000 hiring my team? With that math, one account can more than pay for itself in its first year, and all the rest of the accounts you get from our training become profit. But if I didn't know that information from having asked the question, I wouldn't be able to help the prospect see it from that perspective and justify my cost.

What information do you want to know from your prospects? Think of the problems you or your products solve and figure out what environment would breed those problems. Take a 5-minute break now and quickly write down every question that comes to mind. You can edit them later. Remember, with these questions you aren't trying to find specific problems, it's not time for that in the opening questions. You're just gathering information so that you know exactly where to look for pain when it's time.

Establishing the Need and Unmasking the Pain

Our objective here is to establish that they have a need for what you will offer. If the need never gets established, it's impossible for the sale to happen. In fact, the probability of you making that sale is directly related to the size, scope, and significance of that need. You can interchange the words *need* and *pain*. To put this in perspective, let's reword that sentence. The probability of you making a sale is directly related to the size, scope, and significance of the pain they experience, stemming from the problem you solve.

It's important to remember that there's a difference between a wound and pain. A wound represents a problem but just because someone has a wound, that doesn't mean it always hurts. If we think of what physical pain is, it's an alert system to warn you that something is wrong. Taking a pain killer for example, eliminates the pain but the wound still exists. It's not enough for your prospect to have a wound, they must experience the pain for them to do something about it. In a little bit, I'll show you how to bring attention to the wound and unmask the pain so that your prospect can take action. I use the term unmask instead of create pain because we can't create pain for a wound that isn't there. Either your prospect has challenges, or they do not, but they will never believe in, nor would we ever try to unethically manufacture, a wound that just doesn't exist.

I can tell you that many prospects have problems they're not even aware of, at least they're not aware how serious those problems are. This is because their area of expertise is not in dealing with these types of issues, so they need you to show them the real danger. I remember feeling sick one day but decided to power through my work anyway assuming it was just a cold. As I felt worse, I went to the doctor only to find out that I had walking pneumonia. After that information, I took it more seriously and decided to take the remainder of the day to rest instead. This is the power of a professional opening our eyes to the severity of some of our problems. It's your job to be able to provide that level expertise and educate your prospect on the repercussions of downplaying some of the issues they have.

Not Having to Ask: By easing into the conversation with your initial set of questions, intentionally not going straight for the gold, the prospect feels more comfortable and often will bring up their frustrations on their own. This is a good indication that you are viewed as the authority, you have their trust, and you're in rapport. When that happens, that's wonderful, but our goal here is to build a process that works every time without hoping that the stars align on their own. We know that not everyone you come across will have massive problems weighing on their shoulders, waiting to unload them on you. We also know that some people are guarded, so even if they do have problems they are hesitant to share. In these cases, it's up to you to bring that information out.

The Gentle Ask: If your prospect doesn't bring up their challenges on their own, we can often get that information just by asking a simple general question, "So Jill, I'm curious, what was your motivation for meeting with me today?" You're just trying to understand why they agreed to meet with you. They don't meet with everyone that asks, so there must be a slight level of interest. At the very least you must have piqued their curiosity in some way for them to be willing to take time out of their busy day and agree to share information with you about their company. They aren't doing this for your benefit. They saw some type of opportunity in this or they were thinking about a challenge they have and wanted to see if you can solve it. A good starting point is to find out what they were thinking.

The Direct Ask: At this point, if it didn't come out yet, you have to ask directly. There's a likelihood that your prospect doesn't have a pressing problem that they're thinking about often (or at least one that pertains to your sales conversation). There's still some type of interest, or at the very least, curiosity, but a specific problem may not be in the forefront of their mind. Just for the record, this is not a setback. This is just a way to gauge temperature. Through this process you will increase the heat and get them to that point. Here are a few direct ask questions you can use:

- *What are some of the challenges you experience when it comes to _____?*
- *What do you think is stopping you from _____?*
- *What frustrations do you experience when_____?*

The reason the direct ask comes after allowing them to open up on their own, which, in turn, comes after the gentle ask, is because we don't want to show our cards. If the prospect feels like you're using this information to make a sale, then you break trust. They will no longer trust your intentions because now they'll feel your only goal is to make the sale, not to help them. It's important that you put your prospects and customers first, before your own needs. We all want to make sales, but no sale is more important than the relationship that comes out of it. Also, no sale will ever be more important than your integrity. We know that how they perceive what you're doing is important. To make this work, be truly interested in what they are experiencing, be completely empathetic, and follow this process to the letter every time. Your prospects will have a great experience, you will understand where they are emotionally at all times, and sales will skyrocket.

Strategic Questions: If the previous efforts didn't bring out the wound, we can show the prospect right where to look. With strategic questions, we can go right to the heart of the problems that were identified earlier when we were understanding their world. These questions can completely poke holes in the illusion the prospect has about how perfect their world is. Here's a real example of a process we've developed for a client:

> **Client:** *Bill, you mentioned that things are going well with your current provider. I'm happy to hear that, because service is everything in this business, if your systems aren't properly maintained, machines can go down and your business can grind to*

a halt. Speaking of which, you mentioned that your current vendor comes once every 3 months to check the system. Did you specifically ask them not to come each month to do the maintenance?

Prospect: *No, that's just when they come. They usually come every 3-4 months but most of the time it's every quarter. Should they be coming more often?*

Client: *Yes, and I recommend that you demand that of them. They know they're supposed to be doing it, or at least I hope they know! But if they neglect this then these squeeze tubes go bad and very little soap is pumping into the machine. On top of that, they should be checking the temperature of the water and make sure the programming is right, otherwise you're basically washing your guests' sheets with water. Bad Yelp reviews can dramatically impact your business. Did they give you a super cheap deal on your soap and maybe that's why they cut down on service?*

Prospect: *Definitely not. Their prices have actually risen each of the last two years.*

If we were to bring this up early when the prospect was initially giving this information out, we'd have risked talking about this instead of something that was a big problem for him. We want to focus on things that they already value, before we give them new things to value. Initially, Bill didn't see this as a priority or even a problem and it was only brought up after he thought that everything was great. Now, had Bill started complaining about other issues on his own, the conversation would have been focused on those issues first, and later on we can pile on more reasons they should be making a change.

When asking strategic questions, make sure you're bringing enough challenges to their attention to later justify making a change. In the scenario above, that one pain point won't be enough of a reason to switch suppliers. If enough leverage is built, you can get them to make a change. But if it's not enough, that change may not involve you at all. It may only be getting their current provider to visit more often. Your goal is to establish a critical need and give them enough reasons to make them choose to start a business relationship with you.

I use the term 'establish', because it gives us clear direction as to what we must do. It's not enough for you to grasp the problem, because we have to enable them to *see and feel* the problem and *acknowledge* that it is an issue. Events are neutral: it's the meaning we attach to them that determines the significance. When someone tells me that their company doesn't have a standardized sales process that all their salespeople use, *I* know it's a problem for them. But just because I know, that doesn't mean *they* fully understand the repercussions of what that environment brings. I must ask questions that will help them realize the consequences where they *feel* the need to make a change. It would go something like this:

Me: *John, does the top producer do things differently than your lowest producing salesperson?*

John: *Oh yeah. It's night and day.*

Me: *If your lowest performer did exactly what your top performer did, day in and day out, how much more sales would he bring in?*

John: *Well if Paul did exactly what Lisa did then he'd probably have just as many sales as she does.*

Me: *Out of curiosity, what are their numbers? How much more does Lisa do each year?*

John: *In the last 12 months Lisa generated over $750,000 and Paul generated just under $275,000.*

Me: *Wow!*

John: *Yeah that's not the norm but Lisa beats everyone by at least $200,000 a year.*

Me: *So, what you're saying is with 10 sales reps, your business is missing out on at least $2 million ($200k x 10) a year in revenue because they are not all following the same process Lisa is?*

John: *Yeah, maybe more. I never thought of it that way.*

If I were just to tell John that not having a structured process is a problem without having him realize it on his own, it wouldn't nearly have the same impact. By asking questions, the prospect can come to their own conclusion and a need is firmly established.

Tip: You can use previous prospect Discovery sessions to create killer strategic questions. In one Discovery, I asked the State Manager of a Title Insurance company what their biggest issue in prospecting was and her answer was, that any attorney they would want to do business with would already be established and have relationships with other people. That information helped in another Discovery where the owner told me that business was great, and they didn't have any challenges when it came to sales. When I asked, "How do you deal with the fact that anyone worth targeting already has established relationships?" His answer was that they never figured that out so they stick to their existing relationships. That answer opened the door to many other questions, which ultimately led to a new client. This goes back to the benefit of sticking to a niche. Not only can you leverage your previous successes, but you can leverage your previous Discovery sessions.

Tell Them- But Get Them to Agree: The final approach in establishing a need is to just show them. Obviously, we'd like for them to come to their own conclusion, but when all else fails, then it's time to educate them. Your prospect is smart. If you can help them connect the dots and what you say makes sense, you can establish the need quickly. It's important that we get them to acknowledge the need and agree to what we're saying. You can put words in someone's mouth, but only if you get them to stand behind that statement. Even better, have them expand on it from their perspective.

Summary Statement to Establish Need: Regardless of how you bring the problem out in the open, it's important to simplify it for them in one sentence and get a YES response to establish the need. "So, John, the biggest problem you have is that your team isn't generating enough qualified leads with decision makers. Is that correct?" The simplified sentence should be directly related to what you do so that your prospect can clearly see the need to continue the conversation and potentially have you involved in solving the problem going forward. The power in this summary statement is that it allows you to reframe the information they gave you into a simple problem that you directly solve. The conversation up until this point should be structured so they can agree with your statement as a logical conclusion. Your summary statement to establish the need can be delivered two ways; a statement with a question at the end asking for confirmation (as above), or a statement with a pause at the end waiting for the, "That's right". My personal preference is the statement and then silence until they step in to agree.

> **Side note 1:** The summary statement should only be given when it's obvious they can agree to it. If, for some reason they don't agree with it, then educate them enough until they can see that they have a problem. Do not move forward in the sale until you both agree that a problem they have is a problem you solve.

Side note 2: Notice the above example wasn't framed as, "So, John, the biggest problem you have is that your team isn't generating enough leads". If I were to say that, and we were to establish that as the need, I then open myself up to more competition because anyone selling leads can solve their problem. The key to a powerful summary statement is to frame the problem in a way that you uniquely solve, making you the best candidate. Align your summary statement with your unique selling proposition and you'll have the monopoly on that problem.

Getting Leverage

Fourteen years ago, I was at a Tony Robbins Unleash the Power Within event where he took everyone through what he calls 'The Dickens Process'. If you haven't experienced this for yourself yet, I won't go too much into it because you'll want to do this at some point first-hand, and any description of this powerful process will do it no justice. The exercise gets its name from Charles Dickens' book, *A Christmas Carol*, in which Scrooge is visited by 3 ghosts showing him his past, present, and future. The goal of the exercise is to eliminate your biggest limiting beliefs by building leverage on the pain those beliefs had caused you in the past, present, as well as the damage it's going to do 5, 10, even 20 years into the future if you continue to hold on to those beliefs. Talk about building leverage! Going through this process is an emotional experience where you come out completely committed to change. He asks you questions like, "What has this belief cost you all these years? What has it cost you physically, financially, emotionally?"

The exact questions he asked I don't even remember. What I do remember is the pain that people felt (myself included) and the sounds that filled the room. The only way to describe the sound of thousands of people focusing on their problems, was what you'd imagine Hell to sound like. It was awful. Normally, we make ourselves feel better about the things in our lives that we don't like, and we do this by avoiding the issue and simply focusing on other things. We distract ourselves to escape the real pain because if we don't think about it, we don't feel it. What Tony did was not allow us to escape. He put our focus right on the problem and made us look back to the past, brought us to the present, and asked us to imagine what the future will look like if we continue down that path. As tough as it was to face my reality, that experience was very motivating because I made a commitment, right then and there, that I will no longer tolerate the things in my life that were causing me pain. That's when I had a breakthrough - a lightbulb moment.

I asked myself, if this can have such a profound effect on limiting beliefs, ingrained so deeply in my own psyche, what can it do to the beliefs that hold prospects back from buying? These too are limiting beliefs. When a prospect says, "I can't afford it", can they really afford to not solve the problem? Or when we hear, "That's expensive". Expensive compared to what? What would it cost them five years from now, ten years from now, if they continue to have this problem? My guess is, much more than the price of the product or service we're talking about. As salespeople, it's our absolute responsibility to let the prospect look at the problem honestly and thoroughly so they can make an intelligent decision. By only focusing on what they want to focus on and seeing what they want to see, they risk making a decision that could cause them more pain in the long term, just because it feels better to distract themselves in the moment. Your job is to unmask the pain and ask them to take their head out of the sand. Let them see the reality. And if that reality isn't too bad then there's no need to move forward. But if it is, then you give them an opportunity to create a better future for themselves and their business by fixing it.

The reality is that we all have things we know we know are important, we know we 'should' do and yet we never follow through with. There's only one reason for this. We associate more pain with doing it than not doing it, so we don't take action. And that only happens because we're not thinking about the consequences of not following through. We conveniently forget to consider what the long-term repercussions of inaction are. We allow ourselves to escape the pain by focusing on something different just to feel better. And because things don't *feel* too bad once we escape, we justify not moving forward. Understanding how this works, we can use this in our sales process. If we don't allow our prospects to escape their pain, we can create an emotional experience where they will no longer tolerate their current conditions and possibly put them in a state where they are ready to make a change immediately. Amateur salespeople sell how great their products are, experienced salespeople talk about pain points, but the real pros don't let you escape the pain until you are ready to do something about it.

Here are some leverage-building questions you can ask in your Discovery:

- *Why do you think this problem exists?*
- *How long have you been dealing with this?*
- *What else have you tried to do to fix this?*
- *How does that affect the business?*
- *How do you mean?*
- *Tell me more about that.*
- *If it continues, ultimately what happens?*

- *What's the worst part about that?*
- *Why is that important to you? (Specifically)*
- *Who or what else is affected by this?*
- *What is this costing financially? Emotionally?*
- *How does this affect the department?*
- *Is that a big deal or is that minor?*
- *Why does that matter?*
- *In what way does this affect you personally as the {title} of the company?*

The list can go on and on. If our goal is to help them feel pain by building leverage, going further out in the future magnifies the damage. When we ask what would having that issue cost 5 years from now if it were to continue, that multiplies the loss by 5. For example, if the problem your prospect is experiencing is costing their company $1 million dollars a year in lost sales, that problem not resolved 5 years from now has costed them $5 million dollars in the future. It's always a good practice to get the prospect to quantify the damage whenever possible, even if it's a complete guess. This makes it easier for them to multiply the damage in their mind, therefore experience more pain.

Going further out in the future is especially helpful when your prospect doesn't believe his current situation is all that bad. Remember, we justify things to stay comfortable and that comfort zone keeps us prisoner. It doesn't allow us to move forward. It stops us from creating a better life and, if you allow it, it will stop your prospect from taking action as well. Yes, in this moment the problem might not be so bad. But should your prospect only be concerned about this very moment? Just like a rocket ship only 1 degree off course don't seem like too big of a deal initially.

After 100 yards, you'd only miss your destination by 5.2 feet. But traveling to the moon (the rocket's ultimate destination) it would be 4,169 miles off, nearly twice the diameter of the moon. Ask questions that help your potential customer do the math. Explore scenarios deep into the future, so they can see how far off they'll end up if they don't do something about it today.

I use transportation metaphors a lot when discussing the sales process because when you're selling, all you're actually doing is just moving your prospect from one location to another. From the terrible place they are currently, to their ultimate destination. Your product/service is the vehicle that's going to get them there and you're the driver. You are moving them away from pain and taking them towards pleasure. The bigger the contrast between the two locations, the more likely you are to get a YES from your prospect. Too many salespeople put too much focus on the vehicle (their product) and not nearly enough focus on how dangerous the current environment is that the prospect should be moving away from. Trust me, if you're trying to escape a life-threatening situation, you don't care what the make and model of the getaway car is. Stop selling cars and start selling safety.

Exercise: Write a list of questions you'll use in your Discovery sessions going forward. Remember, people's actions are influenced by how they feel in that moment. And what they feel is influenced by what they are focusing on. You can control what they focus on by the questions you ask. Ask the right questions and you can get them to take the actions you want. Ask the wrong questions and they take the actions you don't

> want. You're the driver, you're controlling where this conversation goes, and potentially if your prospect makes a purchase or decides to pass instead.

Conversation – Not Interrogation

Once we realize how much influence we have over the prospect's purchasing decision, we can easily get so excited that we want to fire off 100 questions but it's critical that your Discovery feels like a conversation and not an interrogation. Notice that I said *feels* like. Although you'll be speaking less and listening more, it's important that you don't make your counterpart feel like their life or business is on display. If they feel like you're going down a checklist of questions, then they'll only want answer questions on a need-to-know basis. If you're selling employee benefit services, for example, you would need to know how many employees they have, and they wouldn't have a problem answering that. But you wouldn't need to know what they fear most about the rising costs of employee benefits. That's what you *want* to know. Yes, getting your prospect to talk about their fears will put them in the best mindset to take action, and yes, that information will tell you exactly where to press if they were to hesitate moving forward, but it's definitely not a need to know. That is just extra information that you'd hope they would share with you.

In a conversation when you have rapport, you'd be surprised how much people will open up to you. But that only happens in an environment where two people are building a relationship and getting to know one another. Each person is building off the previous response in an open dialogue. When your prospect says that they're concerned about the rising costs of benefits, your response of, "What concerns you most about the costs rising?" doesn't seem too intrusive. You are just asking them to clarify their previous statement. And that's why this is called Discovery. You're just trying to discover what is going on in their world. You're trying to understand what's important to them and what's not important to them so that when you present information, you only give the information that they care about most. Seems like common sense, doesn't it? Yet, how common is it for the opposite to happen. Salespeople going on and on about things the prospect doesn't care about, not touching on what they do care about. The truth is they have no idea what's most important because they either never ask or never go deep enough to get to the root issue.

But in order to go deeper, you can't just rattle off questions interrogation style because the prospect will feel like you are overstepping. They'll clam up because you're asking that they expose themselves to you and become vulnerable. The only way they can do this for you is if there's trust. If they feel that you're using this information just to get a sale, trust is gone. Going interrogation style with personal questions will break trust and create an environment where they'll want to give you as little information as possible because they'll be afraid everything they say can, and will, be used against them. This is the exact opposite of everything you want in a sales conversation!

You may be reading this and saying to yourself, George, in an earlier exercise you had me write a list of questions, and now you're saying it's bad to have a list of questions? No, that's not what I'm saying at all. I'm saying it's bad to make your prospect *feel* like you have a list of emotionally provoking questions. It absolutely must feel conversational, spontaneous and genuine, as if whatever they said last had naturally triggered the next question. By now you realize that this whole process is about managing your prospect's feelings. In order to deliver a great experience every time, and to have the highest probability that prospects convert to a sale, we can't hope for the best and just leave it to fate to decide. Hoping that the right questions come to mind at the right moment is not a strategy. We're designing a process that enables us to deliver our best every single time. A process that is repeatable and where the outcome is predictable. We want to methodically plan out each question, then ask those questions in the sequence that will help the prospect feel the specific emotions we want them to feel, and help them move down a path where the obvious conclusion they come to is to purchase your product or service, all without feeling that they're in 'a process'. This is the Speed Path.

When I'm teaching this system to a group, usually about now in the training one of the questions I get is, "If I'm supposed to ask questions and go deep, how do I make it conversational? What do I say in between that keeps the focus on their problem?" It's a valid question because salespeople often want to move on to their presentation since that's when they feel like they're selling. Plus, as human beings we have a natural desire to want to take people out of pain and fix it for them. We must fight both of those urges because it won't help you or your prospect. First, when you're presenting, it's your words telling the prospect they should take action. In Discovery, it is the *prospect's* own words that are telling them they should take action. Who do you think the prospect believes more? Themselves of course. The words you say are being passed through a 'bullshit' filter first. Not everything you say is taken in. What the prospect says, on the other hand, either internally or externally, is automatically accepted as truth. This means, although the Presentation phase feels more like selling, more selling is actually happening during Discovery.

But for Discovery to be effective, we must fight that second urge, wanting to take the prospect out of pain too soon. By wanting to fix it, we're not allowing the prospect to feel the weight of their problems on their shoulders. That is the internal pressure that becomes the catalyst for change. Many people who attempt to create pain unwittingly undo their progress by alluding to possible solutions. This releases the tension and kills any motivation the prospect has to actually do something about it. The feeling that, "I can take care of this any time I want. It's not that bad" happens. And fixing the problem becomes someday in the distant future, along with your sale. This method is designed in a specific way that aligns the buying journey with the sales process to rapidly move the prospect down the path in the shortest amount of time. We are not releasing the tension until right before the Presentation phase. And this only happens once the prospect has made the decision in his or her mind that their current situation is not to be tolerated any longer. At that point, they don't have to be committed to buying from you, but they must decide that the status quo is no longer acceptable. Would it make sense to move on to the Presentation phase at any other point? Why discuss solutions if your prospect doesn't even know if they want to make a change?

This brings us back to the original question; how do we make it conversational, with a natural back-and-forth, if we want to keep them talking and focused on their problems? What can we say if it's our turn to talk and we're not supposed to offer solutions? It actually quite simple: we can add commentary that provokes the situation, we can give, "Uh-huhs" to show we're following along, and we can also tell stories that add fuel to the fire. During Discovery, the prospect will talk a lot more than you and yet they'll feel like they had a great conversation, because it was all about them. They only need to hear your voice occasionally to feel like it wasn't one-sided. Just remember that if they only hear questions from you then their brain will trigger a red flag. But if you mix questions with statements that are right in line with the topic of conversation and throw in some stories of people who were in the same situation, Discovery can go for a very long time.

Side note: In Discovery, make sure not to alleviate the pressure by telling the happy ending to the story. Save that part for the presentation. At this stage keep them in suspense and just help them validate their feelings by talking about others who were in the same shoes.

Exercise: Write a list of problems your existing customers felt before you helped them. Think about all the different emotions they were feeling before, during, and after doing business with you. Have all that information handy (down to the exact phrases they used) so you can make comments that accurately describe what your prospect is feeling. When you get to the point where you can finish their sentences and detail exactly what they're feeling (sometimes down to the words they would use to describe it), they immediately feel that *you get it*. Their thought process is that, if you know this much about the problem, you must have seen it a million times before and most likely you are the best to provide the solution with all that experience. To hammer the point home, imagine the opposite. Imagine going to the doctor and every time you started explaining symptoms you were feeling, he described them wrong. Your pain comes and goes, yet he

---

talks about the pain being constant pain. He describes it as dull and throbbing, but what you feel is very sharp. You wouldn't feel confident in his recommendation because you wouldn't feel that you've been diagnosed properly. The confidence your prospect has in your recommendation, aka your solution, is directly related to how accurately you described the problem and the pain they feel.

Where's the Pain in Pink Cadillacs?

You may sell a luxury product and feel that this process won't work for you. The good news is that it does, regardless of what you sell. Although this book is focused on the B2B market, by no means does that mean that this process is limited to any market or sector. People are people and we instinctively respond the same regardless what is being bought or sold. Someone asked, "What if I sold pink Cadillacs? How would you find the pain in that?" You find the pain first in understanding why they considered purchasing a pink Cadillac in the first place. Remember, people don't buy products, they buy feelings. Your products or services give them an outcome, that's the first thing they buy. But what they really want is what that outcome will do for them. What feeling will that outcome give them? That's what people are searching for and that's what they are buying.

If we can understand what they were trying to get from that purchase, then we know what they are missing. And *that* is where the pain is. Do they want a pink Cadillac because it will make them the talk of the town? If so, why does that matter? You will start to discover the deeper need. Are they considering the purchase as a reward because they work hard? If so, how hard do they work? And when was the last time they've done something for themselves? (I bet it was a long time!) When you go deep, you find pain. See, people keep selling cars when what really needs to be sold is how bad it is to not have what they want, and also, how great it will be to enjoy all the benefits of having what they want. The latter is what we discuss in the Presentation stage and we're almost there.

Establishing that the Timing is Right

If your prospect has a desperate need but doesn't feel that the timing is right, no sale will happen. And it doesn't matter how bad they want what you offer. Timing is *that* important. The great news is that this is completely subjective. It's more about if your prospect *feels* whether the time is right or not, more than it has anything to do with specific circumstances. To make your sales process bulletproof, you must establish that *now* is the time. Of course, these can't be your words, it must be theirs. We do this by asking the right question at the most opportune time to create a knee jerk emotional response, getting the prospect to commit to taking action now. The most opportune time is at the peak of their pain and the right question is, "When are you wanting to fix this?"

Let me say that there's no magic question so don't get too caught up on those specific words, but your goal is to find out when would be the right time to stop all the suffering they just described to you. If you ask at the peak of the pain, the response you typically get is, "Now!" or, "Right away!"

Nobody wants to be the person that just complains about things and doesn't do anything about them. If you ask the timing question at the peak moment, the moment when their fears and frustrations are at a boiling point, the only answer for them to give is that now is the time: the time to draw a line and take a stand that they will not tolerate these conditions any longer. It's time to act!

> **Side Note:** Don't fall into the trap of trying to create too much pain for too long. Eventually this can work against you. We all have a threshold. If the intensity of pain is too great, for too long period of time, our mind will find a way to cope with it and the effect starts to decline. This is a self-preservation mechanism at work. Pain is an alert system in our nervous system set up to warn us and protect us. Once we get the message there's no need to continue to suffer, we tend to reach a fork in the road. We either take action to fix the situation or we just accept the situation and find a way to make ourselves feel better about it. These are two completely different outcomes; the first one leads to a sale and the second one does not. Our goal is to use pain long enough to get them to act and then transition to helping them find pleasure in a better future, a future that involves you. By controlling the narrative, we control the path that enables them to have a set of experiences most likely leading to a purchase.

Their Ideal Future & Buying Criteria

At this stage your prospect has made a mental decision that they are no longer content with what they have, they are ready for something different. This doesn't mean you're the answer, it simply means that the status quo is not. At this point they'd be open to suggestions and would consider what you have to offer because their mind is now in 'shopping for options' mode. As enticing as that seems, it would be premature to make an offer at this stage. We have no idea what they want, which means we have no idea what or how to sell them. Making an offer now means that we're guessing and hoping that our presentation aligns exactly with how they are making their buying decision. To put the odds best in our favor, we'd want to know what their ideal outcome would be and make that our offer (as long as we can provide it).

Imagine going to a restaurant and the server doesn't ask you what you want, but instead, tries to talk you into a hot open roast beef sandwich. And when you explain that you don't want that, they overcome your objection, give you three more reasons why you should eat it, and close you again. That would be silly. What if that was the restaurant's business model and for them to generate revenue (and for people to eat), each server would have to talk customers into a meal of the server's choosing? People wouldn't eat too often! Sales would be extremely low for that business and patrons would have a terrible experience in the process. So why do salespeople try to sell this way? Again, you see it all the time. The salesperson goes on and on about features and benefits that they think are important, but mean nothing to the prospect. Their pitch is filled with a long list of reasons why the prospect should buy, and often covering all but the only reason that matters: the prospect's. Remember, we sell outcomes. We are selling the destination, not the vehicle. So instead of assuming our prospect's destination, we should just ask them what they want, so we don't have to waste time taking shots in the dark.

Creating the Ideal Offer

Buying criteria is how we evaluate one option over another. We all have a customized and highly personal list of those things that are most important to us. These are our values. We determine how good or valuable an offer is based on how they stack up against our list of criteria. We have these value lists for everything. It's what we used to purchase our last vehicle, it's how we choose our spouse, and it's also how you would rate the last prospect you've spoken to. If I were to ask you if your last prospect would be a 'good' customer, you have a set of criteria to determine that answer. It may be how big of a client they can be, how easy they are to deal with, or many other factors you consider. Your prospect also has a value list to determine if *you* would be a good vendor for them. If we know what our prospect is looking for and what they would consider an ideal partner to be, hypothetically we can make sure that our presentation demonstrates those qualities. Understanding what they value most will give us the formula to make the ultimate presentation.

There's a right way and a wrong way to do this. The right way will position you (or your solution) as the best possible choice every single time, while the wrong way will almost always put you in a position to look inferior. Let's first discuss the wrong approach so we can get clear on what *not* to do. **The wrong approach:** *Buying criteria for their ideal vendor- Focusing on you or your company.*

Imagine you were selling digital marketing services and, during a discovery call with a potentially big client you were to ask your prospect, "What's your ideal situation, what are you looking for in a partner?" Based on everything I've said, this question would seem to be in line with eliciting their buying criteria, and this would work well if you fit their criteria exactly, but what happens when you don't? What if they responded that they would want someone who has a lot of experience in dealing with Fortune 500 companies, someone who's been in business for a while, and specifically can point to case studies in commercial banking industry? If your experience doesn't measure up well using that as a gauge, they'll feel you're unqualified. In that case you were better off not asking the question at all because they may not have thought about it. But now that you have asked and they have thought about it, in their eyes you're not the one for them. We never want to ask a question where the answer to that question can possibly kill our chances of making a sale (unless you're at the stage where you are trying to determine if it's a fit. In this example, you're passed that point and are setting up for your Presentation stage). The truth is that, regardless of your experience, using this approach will almost always make you seem unqualified. Why? Because there's so much that's subjective.

What if your firm has plenty of experience serving Fortune 500 companies, but you specifically don't? And how does *he* measure experience? What if you have 3 Fortune 500 clients and he thinks that's not enough? What if you've been in business for 4 years but to him, 'been in business for a while' means at least 10? You could have case studies in commercial banking but he's looking for specific results on specific types of campaigns, and your lack of ability to provide examples that specific may make him feel as if you or your company are not qualified for the job. The wrong approach is to ask what they are looking for in *you*. Remember, you are leading, they are following. They are not qualifying you, you are qualifying them. They're the ones with the problem and in need of help. Not you. You are content. You are the Subject Matter Expert. *You* are determining if you can help them or not. There are hundreds, thousands, or maybe even millions of other businesses that need your help in the world, yet there's only one of you. You couldn't possibly help everyone so you're qualifying them. You're determining if taking them on as a client is a good use of your time, as opposed to filling that slot with someone else.

Most people struggle with this mindset. Unknowingly, they take this powerful sales process and use it against themselves. They think of the pain they have of not having enough customers, or the pressure of not having enough sales, and they feel as *they* are the one with the problem. They look at the prospect as the solution to their pain instead of the other way around. And because of that, they allow the prospect to take control of the relationship. The prospect then fires off qualifying question after qualifying question, while the salesperson desperately hopes to satisfy the prospect with the best answer they can give. Not only is this weak, but it feels terrible for the prospect. Remember, they are coming to you for help on a problem and this robs them of the confidence they should have in you. Which means that even if they do purchase (despite losing trust in your capability) they will constantly question whether they made the right decision. This can lead to buyer's remorse and reneging on the agreement.

Your prospect's ideal future has nothing to do with you or your company. You are simply a vehicle to get them there. There's a time and a place to sell yourself and your company, but that's later in the presentation. At this moment we are setting up the presentation and we want to know what exactly to present. This leads us to **The Right Approach**: *Their ideal outcome.*

The clearer the picture you have of what they want, the more vividly you can deliver that picture when it's time to present. This means the more excited they will be, and that emotion creates desire. When someone wants something bad enough, they'll do whatever they must do to get it. So, a better approach for that digital marketer would be:

> **Salesperson:** *Lisa, if you had a magic wand and you could make anything happen, what impact would marketing have? How would it deliver in a perfect world?*
>
> **Prospect:** *Well, marketing would generate leads for my sales team. They would help us fill up our events. They would just support us better so that sales won't have to do all the heavy lifting.*
>
> **Salesperson:** *If sales had leads coming in with more volume, would that help some of the heavy lifting?*
>
> **Prospect:** *Oh yes definitely!*
>
> **Salesperson:** *Tell me more about the events you want to fill.*
>
> **Prospect:** *This is something we've wanted to do for a long time, but we haven't really figured that part out yet. We'd love to be able to do events in all major cities. We have great ideas for keynote speakers.*

The magic behind this is that you open possibilities for them. This becomes exciting. You can keep this going by asking who they would love to have as speakers. With questions like these you open their mind and they start talking about things that would not normally come up in a traditional sales call. When you do this, they are no longer 'shopping' in their mind. You are asking them to dream and to imagine they can have anything they want. For that little moment, they have hired you and together you two are exploring where this relationship can go. They're dipping their toe in the water and seeing what their future would look like with you involved.

Because we control the questions, we control what they focus on in their mind, and because of this we control what they'll feel. When we repeatedly ask the magic question, "Why?" we get everything we need to make a compelling presentation. You can ask the magic question in many ways and the deeper you go, the stronger the emotional strings you tug on.

Very similar to the process to elicit the pain, we use the process to elicit pleasure:

- What do they want?
- Why do they want it?
- How come that is important?
- What do they ultimately get by having that?

The answers to questions like these show you exactly what benefits to focus on later in your presentation. Going back to the example earlier about salespeople typically talking about what they think is important, now you'll be able to speak to the topics that are directly linked to their desires or fears - their key drivers. While your competitor is talking about their 'innovative platform', you can talk about how great it's going to feel when she is recognized for filling the events that no one else in her department has been able to fill, and what her department will now be able to achieve with hot qualified leads being delivered to her salespeople daily.

Having your prospect picture themselves in the future and experiencing a situation they desire is a technique taught in NLP called Future Pacing. The power in this technique is *how* we use it and where it's strategically placed in our sales process. At this point, the prospect has now decided they must take action, but they haven't decided with whom. We are the first to bid for the job, as it just so happens, and this new window of opportunity opened up while we're right in the middle of a conversation with the prospect. (Lucky us!) Instead of trying to sell ourselves while the prospect is in shopping mode, we hijack their mind and immediately give them a rush of dopamine as they visualize a perfect future. Bids are over. You won. There's no need to go to anyone else as long as you can make what they visualized a reality. Proving you can deliver is in Presentation.

Ideal Offer

Before we wrap this segment up, I'd like to add one last component to the ideal future. Although the primary goal is to discuss ideal outcomes and to get a clear picture of your prospect's underlying desires, an additional opportunity presents itself in the process. You can actually have the prospect build their perfect offer. This differs based on the industry you're in and the products or services you provide. If your industry is commoditized, then your opportunity to differentiate is contingent on the level of service you're willing to deliver. Asking about their ideal future, when it comes to doing business with a company like yours, gives you an opportunity to find out what it will take to win the business. If they tell you that they'd ideally love a call once a week to check in on them, and their business is worth that effort, then you will make that an official part of your offering in the Presentation stage. Your competitor won't think to ask and may not even bring up how often they'll check in on the prospect because they don't know it's important to them. And if they do happen to bring up that topic, they have no idea what the prospect's preference is because they never asked. They might offer a check-in call twice a month or twice a week. Either way it's either too little or too much. Your offer is just right.

If you provide a range of products and services, and your offering is custom to each client or situation, then this is where you and the prospect can start building the package together. By having them engaged in the process, they are emotionally involved, have ownership in the project, and are equally invested. They are just as interested in seeing this come to fruition as you are. An offer that was built to meet the specific needs of the prospect, and designed by the prospect, is a very hard offer for the prospect to refuse.

Last Tips on Discovery

Inbound vs Outbound Discovery: Your Discovery process will be slightly different depending on how the lead was generated. Inbound and outbound have different strengths. The strength of outbound is that you can target the exact companies who would be perfect for your offering, target the specific people at those companies who have the authority to make the decision, get them early in the buying process so you'll have virtually no competition, and generate leads at a much lower cost per lead. The strength of inbound is that the prospect is coming to you, so you are in more of a power position. If you used an outbound lead generation strategy to create interest, the prospect may be open to exploring the possibilities with you but not necessarily have a need. This is why we build our discovery to quickly find the need and help them see it. When someone calls in or fills out a web form, they are already coming to you with a need. You won't have to understand their world or spend the time trying to establish a need. After initially connecting with them, you can jump right into the pain with phrases like, "So tell me what's going on" or, "How can I help?"

This Discovery process is very powerful, and it also works extremely well on inbound leads. Since you hold the power when a prospect comes to you, there's no power struggle or need to establish your authority. It's already there. Because of this, you can be much more forward when amplifying the pain. You can ask questions that you may not normally feel as comfortable asking. Since they are literally asking you for help, it may give you the extra confidence to press on the wound.

Prepare your Discovery Questions: This is a process that will allow you to manufacture feelings in your prospects, therefore manufacture new customers. Anyone in the manufacturing industry can tell you that consistency is most important. To create a predictable process, you will want to have a structured set of Discovery questions that you ask at specific points of the conversation as you go down this assembly line. Do not make the mistake of thinking that you will be successful winging it. Yes, it can work sometimes but it won't be optimal. Every deviation from the optimal process reduces your probability of closing the prospect. And like a casino, your revenue is tied to that probability. Winging it is just throwing money away.

Simple Sale vs Complex Sale: Complex sales are typically associated to larger ticket purchases, where smaller purchases typically require simple sales processes and revenue is made up in volume. If you are selling a high cost product or service, then I suggest that you prepare for each Discovery call individually by adjusting some of your standard questions to that meeting. This way you can ensure that the best questions will be asked for that complex scenario. Doing some research on the individuals and companies you will be speaking with can give you great information to ask great questions. Simple sales on the other hand would not need that level of customization or attention since it may not be a good return on investment of your time and effort.

Summary:

Connect: Before every stage connecting comes first. It's not just rapport. The prospect must be on the same wavelength as you. One of your tasks is to establish a connection. Then, and only then can you move forward. Just like the internet, without a connection the information will not transfer.

Establish the Need: Find the problem that they have and let them see it. This must be a problem that you can solve and perfectly matched with what you plan on offering. If you have many different solutions to choose from then you can allow this part of the conversation to flow more organically because whatever problem they have, you have a solution for. If you sell only one product or there's only one specific option, then you will narrow your path by narrowing your questions to bring out the specific challenges your product addresses. Before moving on to the next step, it's important that you establish that your prospect has a need. They must see it and agree that a problem exists.

Intensify the Pain: How fast they move will be determined by how *big* of a problem they have. The only way they perceive the size of that problem is by the intensity of the pain they feel. If they feel a lot of pain, their brain says this is a big problem and your prospect will be quick to act. If they don't feel pain, then you're only relying on enticing them with pleasure. Pleasure can be a tremendous motivator but why use only half of your arsenal? Press on the pain, let them feel it. Amplify it by helping your prospect look far into the future so they can associate that the longer they have this problem, the more it will cost them. That association makes them realize that the faster they act, the more they can salvage from loss.

Establish the Timing is Right: If you did the above correctly, then they'll agree that now is the time to do something about the problem they have. It's important that they come to that conclusion on their own. We make this happen by asking, at the peak of their pain, when they are urgently wanting to fix the issues they've just described. If you created enough pain and you asked at the right moment, fixing those issues becomes a priority for them. In 'Intensify the Pain' you've helped them realize that delaying will only make things much worse and they'll tell you that they want to fix the problems now. If you skip this one question to establish timing, you are risking the prospect not completing the sale because of a timing issue. At some point in their decision-making process, they will contemplate if now is the appropriate time to do this. So why not control when that thought process happens and strategically place it at the point of the conversation that has the highest odds of getting a YES?

Ideal Outcome: We use future pacing to amplify pleasure as they talk about their perfect future. This is all about the destination, where they want to go. We want to know what their ideal future would look like, so we can offer that specific outcome and visual in our presentation stage. A ton of great things are happening during this exercise from the science of influence perspective. For them to paint this picture for you, they must imagine it. As they imagine it, they experience all the positive emotions that come with that picture, and they are anchoring those positive feelings to doing business with you. They are also telling you what's most important to them. If we're selling destinations, not vehicles, then you get to find out their ultimate destination and offer it to them. Finding out their ideal outcome will give you the key to their hearts and minds. It gives you the formula to create the best presentation possible. And by best, I mean best for them. While other salespeople are poking around hoping to hit a hot button, you'll be able to hit it every time just repeating their own words back to them.

Ideal Offer: Find out what they'd ideally like from *you*. This must be done after you've discussed their Ideal Outcomes so it's not a question of qualifying you. At this point they already want you and now it's just what they'd like you to deliver. If they don't know too much about the products or the services you provide, then you can skip the ideal offer because they won't have one in mind. You will educate them in the Presentation stage as to what is the ideal offer looks like. Hint... it's the one you give them! On the other hand, if working with a company like yours is pretty standard and they know what to expect, have them tell you what they would like you to provide for them. This will become your official offering in your presentation.

Resource: Submit your Discovery questions for a review. We will selectively choose submissions and those chosen will be given our analysis on your Discovery document. You will get our feedback and suggestions so that you have a kickass discovery process. To submit your discovery questions, go to: www.client-machine.com/discoveryreview

Chapter 12

Presenting

Over the last two decades of training and working with sales-people, I can tell you that the Presentation stage is where sales-people typically spend most of their time. This is the part of the sales conversation where the traditional sales pitch comes in. You're selling yourself, your company, and your product or ser-vice. You're describing features, explaining benefits, presenting your offering, maybe even giving a demonstration. There are many reasons salespeople spend an inordinate amount of time in the Presentation stage and most of those reasons have to do with the old-school approach to sales. For example, the tradi-tional belief has been that the buyer is the one in control. Since the buyer has the money, the traditional view has been that he or she holds the power. And from that perspective, the salesper-son would give their best pitch while the buyer sits back in their chair waiting for the salesperson to convince them it would be a good investment. It's like a bad episode of Shark Tank. You can just picture Mark Cuban saying, "You haven't convinced me, that this would make me money, yet."

Hopefully this book has, so far, done a good job of giving you a new perspective: a perspective where you're in the chair and hold all the power. But that new perspective is only a starting point. It's the process that gives you the necessary framework to maintain control and keep the power on your side. See, the reason this went on for so long is that the old school belief fed right into the second reason people spend a disproportional amount of time presenting: people love talking about themselves. It's just human nature. And when people are talking about how great their company is or how amazing their products are, it's the just an extension of their desire to talk about themselves. Unfortunately, because of this, most salespeople just talk, talk, talk all the way through and out of a sale. In your new Discovery process, you are going to use that very human nature to work in your favor, allowing the prospect to do most of the talking, and therefore talking themselves *into* a sale.

The third reason salespeople spend most of the sales conversation presenting, is because they've always been told that this is what selling is, when in fact, it's only one stage of a process. So, for years salespeople have been taught to just, "Sell" and that, "Sales is just a numbers game." Which really means, *don't ask your prospects what they want or care about, just talk about how great you are. And if you repeat that terrible process often enough, you will eventually stumble across people who will find what you're talking about appealing.* You could imagine why this approach yields very low conversion rates, and why salespeople eventually get burned out. The other day I was watching the movie "The Founder" and in the beginning, it shows Michael Keaton, playing Ray Kroc, lugging a milkshake machine from restaurant to restaurant, making the same presentation over and over, trying to find someone to buy it. I thought to myself, this is what many salespeople are still doing today, with the only difference being they are now using the telephone or email. For many, sales has only evolved by using technology to make more contacts, which serves only to compensate for their bad sales process by doing more volume. The numbers game mentality strikes again.

Sales has gotten marginally more sophisticated for others as they've incorporated a consultative approach to their process. The problem is that it's just not enough. Yes, it's better than Roy Kroc's approach but if you don't go deep enough it just won't be enough to move a prospect. There is a major shift that's been happening because of technology, where buyers are getting more information about products and services from websites and videos, having less contact with salespeople. More of the buying decision is happening without you. Marketing is taking over more functions that have traditionally been given to sales, which also means that buying behaviors are changing. With buyers getting more of the information they need through these other avenues, sales is often coming in on the tail end of the transaction. The less salespeople are involved in the whole process, the smaller the opportunity we have to influence the sale. This is especially true with leads that are generated by inbound. At least outbound you can create interest and have a sales conversation before the prospect is shopping for it on their own time.

But this shift in power from salesperson to prospect will continue and that gap will widen as technology gets more sophisticated. For example, chatbots are using Artificial Intelligence and they're having conversations like humans. It's a matter of time before they take over a bigger portion of the buyer's journey, leaving you only a tiny window of opportunity to influence the outcome. What this means for the salesperson is that you have to use every strategy, tactic, and tool that gives you an edge to combat this transition of power. No longer can we rely on what is currently being taught in sales. As technology gets more sophisticated, so must our sales process. The principles in this book can help you regain that edge. I'm hopeful that others in the field build on these principles, so we can take the science of sales even further.

The Presentation Stage Defined

As we dive into the formula for making powerful presentations, let's start by explaining exactly how and from which previous step we would be entering this stage of the process. If you have a simple sale and you are using the 'One Call Close' approach, then you are simply moving the conversation from Discovery to Presentation during the same call or meeting. If you have more of a complex sale or selling a more expensive package, then you may want to split up these sales conversations into multiple meetings to avoid making the prospect feel like they're making a rush decision for such a big purchase. In that case, going into this Presentation stage would start as a new call or face-to-face appointment. For those of you selling very large products or services, you may have multiple Discovery sessions and multiple Presentations before the deal is sealed.

Regardless how this phase is broken up, the principles of each phase, and the goals outlined, will always be the same. For your Presentation to be effective, it's important to focus on outcomes and fight the urge to get stuck on the details. This seems counterintuitive because details are what we would think the prospect needs to make a buying decision, but nothing could be further from the truth. The decision we want them to make is whether or not they would like an outcome we are offering. It's selling the destination over the vehicle. How you get to that destination is not nearly as important. They are not evaluating if they want your web design services, they're evaluating if they want a cutting-edge website that positions their company as a leader in their field. That's what they're deciding, that's what you are offering them, and that's what they will get by hiring your company. Once they agree they want that outcome, then you can show them the specifics on how you will get them there. At that point they're sold, you just have to prove you can deliver.

Your Big Promise

Your big promise is exactly what it sounds like, the big outcome you promise to deliver, summed up in one powerful sentence. This quick summary immediately tells the prospect where this conversation is headed and creates the interest needed for them to listen to the details. Think about how you read a newspaper. You don't read every word in every article, do you? That would be painful. It also wouldn't be realistic because you wouldn't spend all that time reading things that didn't interest you. Instead, you skim through the headlines and find the one that compels you to read. That headline is your big promise. Not only do headlines summarize what you'll get from reading that article, but the headline is what sells you on reading it. Headlines are specifically written in a way to grab your attention. In fact, if it didn't grab your attention, you wouldn't spend another moment reading that article further. The same goes for your big promise. This is your opportunity to sell the story. If your promise is big enough, bold enough, and speaks directly to the need that they have, it will compel them to listen to every last detail of your pitch. On the contrary, if your big promise isn't promising enough, there isn't any real motivation on their end to listen to what you have to say.

The key to making a powerful Big Promise is that it describes the prospect perfectly and also describes the specific outcome the prospect is looking for. How do we know what specific outcome the prospect is looking for? We asked in Discovery. Not only did we ask, but we also summarized all the prospects needs in one easy to deliver package with our Summary Statement. The example we used earlier was, "So, John, the biggest problem you have is that your team isn't generating enough qualified leads with decision makers. Is that correct?" Your Big Promise speaks directly to that and it can be something like, "We help midsize companies generate hot qualified leads with hard to reach decision makers, so they can rapidly grow sales." By speaking to their biggest problem, it says, "We're not perfect for everyone but we're perfect for people with your problem". Be the king of that hill - that's the only hill that matters.

Now, if you were in the lead generation business could it also be true that you help small companies, or large companies? Sure. Does it matter? Not to this prospect. Do you maybe have other services that you provide other clients? Yes, but does that matter? Not here, not right now. Your Big Promise is delivered to the specific prospect you're talking to and offers the specific outcome that prospect is looking for, nothing more, nothing less. And by starting off your presentation this way, you immediately grab their attention, giving you a captive audience, hanging on your every word.

Selling Your Company and Yourself

Since you just made a big bold promise, now would be a good time to back those words up by giving your prospect confidence in your company's ability to perform. Making bold statements without validation just feels like hype. This is your opportunity to quickly demonstrate that you can deliver on your promise, and that they won't have to listen to this whole presentation, only to find out at the end that you've never done this before. Just like the Big Promise, this allows your prospect to see that it's worth investing the time to hear you out.

Earlier, we said that in order for the information to transfer from you to your potential new customer, there must be a connection between the two of you. That connection requires rapport and must be established in every conversation or interaction. When we have rapport, the prospect knows, likes, trusts, and respects us. This becomes their opportunity to do all the above.

It's important to note that we don't need to spend a ton of time selling ourselves here. The last thing our prospects want to hear is for us to go on and on about how great our company is, how many awards we won, and any self-proclaimed titles created by our marketing departments. The prospect wants to hear just enough to know that you can fulfill that big promise, then they want you to move on to a more interesting topic: what you can do for *them*. Does this mean that they don't want to hear about your awards or big-name clients that you throw around? No, these are important and can be a powerful tool. Just know that the only reason you are mentioning these things is to establish that you can help *them* and that you can deliver on your promise. If you are mentioning awards that have nothing to do with the task at hand or you are mentioning big name clients that look nothing like the prospect's company, then you're not proving that you can deliver the specific promise you made *them*. Make sure your examples are relatable.

> **Side Note:** If you are going to give some background on both you and your company, start with your company first. This gives a 30,000-foot view and moves down. If your personal background or expertise can add value to the relationship, then mention it. But if not, I recommend moving on to what matters most to the prospect and save that for another time.

Features, Benefits, Benefits, and More Benefits

For us salespeople, it becomes easy to get stuck on features. Since we are experts in our own market, we understand the significance of statements like, "85 high-resolution pages per minute" or how big a deal 'same-day service' may be in our world. But does your future client really understand the difference? They may at the surface, but do they really *feel* the difference? By now it's obvious that this whole process is about inducing and directing feelings. Too often sales presentations are filled with talk of features which have very little emotional impact. It's our responsibility to connect the dots for the prospect so they can understand how those features will make their life better. And although many times the benefits seem obvious, unless the prospect plays it out in their mind, they won't *feel* the benefit. Let me give you an example.

If someone were to say to you, "We have a money-back guarantee". Doesn't the benefit seem obvious? So obvious that it almost feels like there's nothing more to say on the matter. And because it's that obvious, often, nothing more is said. But what if instead they were to say, "We offer a 100% no questions asked money back guarantee. Which means that if you don't find the program valuable, it costs you nothing. Just let us know within 30 days and we'll refund your entire investment. You have nothing to lose and everything to gain". Now doesn't that feel different from just mentioning the guarantee? To the prospect who's on the fence, you bet it does. Was anything else offered? Nothing, other than a compelling visual that allows them to experience the full benefit of your offer.

Too often we allow the 'obvious' to limit us from delivering the feeling the prospect wants, and needs, to make a buying decision. What's obvious to us is not obvious to the prospect. Same-day service doesn't mean anything until you can give them a visual of their equipment going down in the middle of the business day, and operations coming to a halt until a service technician arrives. They simply can't appreciate the gift you are offering with same-day service until they can imagine what it would be like when they need it most. The same goes for all the features we speak on; our audience won't be able to fully appreciate the value until we provide some context and emotion.

It's often said in sales that people don't buy drills, they buy quarter-inch holes. But let's take that analogy one step further. People don't buy quarter-inch holes, they're buying the feeling they will have enjoying their new 75-inch TV that's being put on the wall or the significance they'll feel when they pull off the big event they are wiring the venue for. See, it's so much deeper than outcomes. It's what that outcome really offers in the grand scheme of things and the feelings that come with that future. Realistically, the drill is just a tool, and so is your product or service. It's just a tool to get a specific outcome. So, at the very least we can't sell drills, and we know that. But I want to argue that we can't sell holes either. We must take it even further than what's traditionally taught in Feature-Benefit selling. To continue with the metaphor, let's talk about the person who buys a drill to make a hole to hang up that television. Do they really care about holes? Will that give them the emotional charge we want? Of course not. They're all excited about watching the big game on that big TV, so their Super Bowl Sunday party is talked about for years, or whatever the specific scenario is. It's the compelling futures they envision that excites them enough to buy. This is why we must move past Solution Selling and move to *Destination Selling*. We are helping the prospect move away from pain, and drive towards pleasure so they can ultimately get to their happy place. Your solution is just the vehicle that transports them from one place to the other. We are not selling vehicles, which means we are not selling solutions.

I capitalize Destination Selling, not to create a new buzz word, but to give clear direction for what is needed to be done, which is to sell the destination. This is what their life will look like, feel like, and ultimately be like far out into the future as a result of this purchase. During the Discovery phase, our prospect described what they were moving away from and what they want to move towards. Now in the Presentation phase, it's our responsibility to offer a clear picture of where they'll end up. The decision to choose us over our competitor is simply to choose the destination we are offering over theirs. Using the process described in this book, you'll be light years ahead of your competitors for two reasons: First, very few people even know they should be selling destinations. Most people are stuck on features, a few mention some benefits, and almost no one takes benefits as far into the trajectory that I'm suggesting. Second: even if your competitor started selling destinations tomorrow, you will always offer the better destination. How can we be so sure? Because we had the prospect describe in detail their ultimate destination during our discovery process.

So here's a great example. For the sake of brevity, let's imagine someone just gives us direct, honest, and blunt answers without the niceties or etiquette that would be required in a real-life conversation.

Prospect: *My website feels old*

You: *Why does that matter?*

Prospect: *It hasn't been changed in years so it's more like a brochure and not as interactive as I'd like.*

You: *Why does that matter?*

Prospect: *Because I think visitors aren't staying on it long enough and when someone is on it for a while, there's no way for me to capture their information.*

You: *Why does that matter?*

Prospect: *Because I'm not generating leads.*

You: *Why does that matter?*

Prospect: *Because I'm working so hard to generate sales, it kills me to think that I'm wasting opportunities that I could be capturing from that traffic!*

This can obviously continue on and on. Without leads there are no sales. Without sales there's no revenue. Without revenue there's no business. Without a business there's a significant life change. The deeper you go, the clearer the destination they want. By the way, we also had asked them to describe their ideal outcome. Understanding their pain (what they don't want) and knowing their ideal future (what they do want), you have everything you need to create the ultimate destination. So now lets' go back to your feature, benefit, benefit, and more benefits using only the above information.

Telling the prospect above that you will create a new website is just the starting point. A new website is just a feature. We want them to see what they're really getting from that project. A good way to connect the dots for your prospect would be to imagine they ask you the magic question, "Why does that matter?" after everything you say. With this approach, you move from features to destinations. It may sound something like this:

One of the things we would do for you is create a brand-new, custom-designed interactive website. Not only will it look and feel new and innovative, but it will be very interactive, so visitors will engage more and stay on it for a while. And we both know that the longer they're on it, the more likely they are to eventually buy from you. The new site will have many ways to capture visitor information so that you can generate leads from the all the traffic you're already getting. With a regular flow of leads being generated, you will finally be able to grow sales and generate more revenue. Not only that, but you won't have to work so hard doing it because instead of your website operating like an outdated online brochure, your new website will operate like a virtual salesperson, generating leads for you.

This feels completely different from the prospect's perspective. It's like magic to their ears. Talk about offering the perfect destination. It creates the feeling of, "This person gets me". Not only does this go far beyond features and benefits, but you've touched on all the things that are important to them, and only those things! While your competitor is talking features, you are talking about what matters. And this is why it's important to dig deep in Discovery. Imagine if the prospect said that their website felt old and you didn't dig deeper. On the surface, it doesn't seem like there's any reason to go further. Prospect feels like their website looks old and they want a new one. Great, got it. But we can just have easily assumed that the *problem* with having an old site is that it makes the company look inferior to their competitors. And although that is also true, that was not the concern for this imaginary prospect. Spending time fixing that problem would not have done much for you.

Sales are lost when assumptions are made. We want to fully understand what our prospects don't want (moving away from) and what they do want (moving towards). Why they want it and why that is even important. As we go deeper into the pain, we can go further along the trajectory when offering pleasure. Their deepest fear gives us insight to their greatest desire. The amount of information you can extract determines how fantastic a destination you can offer.

Every single feature you discuss should be tied to the outcomes they want. Continuing the example above, if your offering also consists of marketing automation, you would tie it to the fact that the prospect feels they are working too hard. Without spelling it out for them they will not *feel* the benefit. Every time you tie a feature to the benefits they are specifically looking for, it builds the bridge from where they are today to where they want to be. Promising to take them to their ultimate destination is no longer some pie-in-the-sky promise, they can actually see how you will get them there step-by-step, one feature at a time.

> **Side Note:** Leave out the features and benefits that don't mean anything to the prospect. Again, while other salespeople are pressing random buttons hoping they touch a hot button here or there, you're just pressing hot button after hot button until the prospect says YES.

> **Side Note:** Knowing the magic words to say doesn't mean that you should always say them. At the risk of sounding annoying, I just want to mention once more not to promise anything you won't or can't deliver on. This process will give you the ability to generate the clients you want, so do just that. Go after the right ones and leave the others behind. The power behind this process is that you no longer have to settle for those who aren't a fit. When demand is high, you can pick and choose who you want to work with. You have control of your demand, therefore control of who you let in. Don't make the mistake of overpromising something you can't deliver, taking on clients that aren't perfect for your organization. With this system it's easy to tell someone exactly what they want to hear because you know exactly what that is. It's okay to tell someone what they want to hear, in fact, that's the whole point of this, but just make sure it's true. Because the real point in learning this is to create long-lasting business relationships and lying is the easiest way to destroy one.

Spice Things Up – Season Your Pitch

Adjectives and Adverb

The words you use will determine the intensity of emotion your prospects feel. One of the keys to making a *killer* presentation is to season your pitch with adjectives and adverbs that create vivid and stimulating visuals. What feels better, a sales pipeline or a *massive multimillion-dollar* sales pipeline? A way to get more clients or a system that *consistently* generates new clients *each week*?

When presenting, our goal is to take our prospect on an emotional journey where they are so excited they're hanging on our every word. We want our words to captivate our audience where nothing matters around them, where time just flies because our message is so compelling. It becomes easy to use the shortest amount of words to describe what we're trying to describe but this short ride isn't the scenic route. The scenic route is what will evoke the emotions conducive to buying. Adjectives and adverbs bring more information to the table, describing your offering in more detail. How can we expect our prospect to buy if we are not demonstrating the full value of our offering and robbing them of the emotional experience that they deserve?

Metaphors

Another great way to spice up your presentation is to use metaphors. A metaphor is a symbol that carries with it all its associations and brings those associations right into the conversation. If I were to say to you that this process will add *rocket fuel* to your sales, you kind of get the picture. And that's the point. A few well-chosen words can have a huge impact by creating vivid and exciting pictures.

Metaphors also offer a shorthand form of learning. If you showed a child a picture of cow and then said the word 'cow' they would learn the name of that animal by associating the picture with the word. The same goes for your products or services. Your prospects can quickly 'learn' what your product will do for them by associating the picture the metaphor creates with your product. This picture is a quick peek into their future, a powerful glimpse of the destination ahead.

Stories

Each one of these 'seasoning' techniques will take your presentations to a whole new level. But by far, my favorite is story-telling. A story allows you to make a statement without making a statement. It gives you the opportunity to get a point across by *demonstrating* rather than telling. This is an important distinction because not everything you say will be taken at face value when you're 'telling'. There's always a bit of skepticism as a new relationship is being established. In the beginning, trust is at the all-time low. As you perform over time, trust increases, and the skepticism diminishes. This is true in all relationships but especially when dealing with salespeople.

When you're telling a story, your audience can get lost in it like a good movie. They can put themselves in the shoes of the protagonist and experience everything that character experiences. As they become lost in the story, they can take in your entire message without their overprotective bullshit filter reducing it down to nothing. This filter naturally exists within all of us and is there to protect us. But all too often it robs us of a great experience in the name of safety. It can go too far for our own good. Although we can be 'safe' from the outside world by never leaving the house, would it really be worth it? Similarly, our fear of making a bad decision or our fear of being taken advantage of can be so great that this bullshit filter can deprive us of amazing opportunities and experiences. I describe it as overprotective because this isn't something we are consciously choosing to do. This defense mechanism is stepping in on our behalf and often interjecting itself where it doesn't belong.

Our prospects can validate our claims later, but for now we want them to accept what we're saying at face value and have a great experience in the process. Realistically, if anything we present didn't check out at the end or we couldn't back up our claims, the deal would die anyway so their bullshit filter isn't necessary. Since we can't just ask them to shut it off, a good story will bypass it, not by directly asking them to believe our statements, but by just listening to what happened to others who were faced with similar problems and choices. A good story will captivate your audience and allow them to see how their own story will play out through the eyes of another person. It's almost as if they get to try you before they buy you, allowing someone else to buy first and seeing what happens. The good news is that they don't have to wait for success to happen, it already has.

So, what would we consider a good story? A good story depicts a real-life scenario of an individual who has a similar circumstance to your prospect, and tells what happened before, during, and after that individual purchased your product or service. It vividly describes how that person was feeling in all three of those stages so that the prospect can have a similar experience as they simulate the purchase in their mind. Since the main character in your story is feeling exactly what your prospect is feeling now, you can change how they feel by leading them to a different place, vicariously through the character. In fact, the better that your story can match the prospect's world, the more impact it will have.

Imagine being able to describe a case study where your existing client was in the same exact place as your prospect. She was dealing with the same problems, worried about the same things. She had the same reservations in making a purchase as your prospect but for whatever reason your client decided to move forward anyway. Now she's grateful that she took action in spite of her fear because her business and life are better now as a result of it. This journey from fear to appreciation can create a parallel experience in your prospect. A story that's similar in circumstance and accurately describes how your prospect currently feels can create a future memory, where they not only see how the end plays out, but they also experience all the positive emotions that happy ending creates. Stories can be used in any stage of your sales process but they are especially powerful when they're used in the Presentation stage and Overcoming when you're dealing with objections.

Your Secret Sauce

In a world full of options, it's becoming increasingly challenging to choose one solution over another in the market. There's a good chance your competitors are continuing to create this confusion by not differentiating themselves from the rest. Most are being generalists instead of specialists, trying to appeal to everyone yet appealing to no one. Day in and day out they're repeating the same marketing message that everyone else is using in the industry. Even worse, marketers are suggesting that the way to compete in this madness is by creating *more* content than their counterparts. Which means, content pushing the same message is then recycled, repackaged, and repurposed in an attempt to drown out the others, furthering this insanity. Who's suffering from all this?

For one, your competitors are, but who cares? They deserve it since they're responsible for creating this environment, but take a minute to think about your prospect, who's completely frustrated during their time of need. Here they are with a problem, trying to make an informed decision yet there's no way to make any comparison because everyone is saying the same thing. For us, this environment gives us a huge advantage since we're focused on dominating specific niches and creating powerful personalized value propositions. With our approach, we are creating specific messages to specific people, who have specific pain points and offering those people specific solutions and outcomes that are customized for each individual. That's pretty damn specific.

Now it's time to take it one step further by *owning* the best way to solve our prospect's problem. We own it by not only having the best way to solve our prospect's problem, but with a solution that is proprietary. This can be a patented formula, a proprietary technology, a unique methodology, exclusive rights, or a unique set of skills. In other words, even if everyone in the world copied every single thing you did, they can't copy this. Your secret sauce is unique to you and nobody has this differentiator in their possession. By *owning* the best way to solve the problem, you have a monopoly on the only real solution to that problem. Everything else is a knock-off.

While your competitors compete on price, you're not competing at all. They're not in your league. There's you and then there's everyone else. Your secret sauce puts you in a class all by yourself. Do you remember earlier when we said you are in the position of power, not your prospect? That there's an entire globe filled with prospects but only one of you? Well, your secret sauce is the very reason you can come from power and that there *is* only one of you. Your secret sauce is the monopoly on the best way this problem is solved, it's the ultimate solution. They can't get it anywhere else, regardless of how competitors try to push their knockoffs.

Make sure your presentation demonstrates that your secret sauce is by far the best solution to their problem *and* that there is no comparable alternative. It's worth your time describing how that magic formula was discovered or developed because it's the story behind your secret sauce that creates the magic. Your product or service becomes so exciting, so interesting, so fascinating that it almost becomes this mystical key to your prospects ideal future. Think I'm exaggerating? Create an origin story for your secret sauce. Tell everyone about it and watch how they respond to you. You'll be amazed.

Summary:

Big Promise: Start off your presentation with the specific outcome they're looking for. This is a continuation of your summary statement. Your big promise shows that you deliver specific results for specific people. The results and people match the prospect perfectly.

Selling Yourself and Company: Sell your company first then sell yourself, if and only if, you matter in the relationship. This is a short, sweet description that should last less than 60 seconds. It's just to let the prospect know they won't be wasting their time hearing your pitch. It validates your big promise and creates the motivation for your prospect to go to the end.

Features, Benefits, Benefits, and More Benefits: Attach a value to each feature you mention by helping the prospect understand why it's important. Let them see how each feature will benefit them in the short, medium, and long term. Allow them to visualize the domino effect that happens as a result of each feature you mention. The bigger the ripple and the further out in the future you describe, the more impact each feature has emotionally. Resist the urge to cut your explanation short. Assume the prospect has no idea what the benefits are, regardless how obvious.

Spice Things Up – Season Your Pitch: Use adjectives, adverbs, metaphors, and stories in your presentation to create an emotional charge. Nouns and verbs alone are boring, **adjectives and adverbs** give it context, create a better visual, and intensify the emotional impact of your words. **Stories** allow you to take the prospect on an emotional journey, allowing them to see how things play out through the eyes of someone who has already purchased from you. Stories are emotional, powerful, and bypass more of the bullshit filter than your statements. **Metaphors** are like a combination of the previous two. They are a mini story that gives context to your statement when the two are compared. Spice up your presentation by evenly sprinkling adjectives, adverbs, metaphors and stories throughout your pitch like seasoning.

Your Secret Sauce: If the *best* way to solve your prospects problem is done using a method or tool that is *proprietary*, then you have a monopoly on solving that problem. For your secret sauce to have a huge impact, it's important that you show both of those elements; that it's the most effective way to solve it and that no one else has this specific method. If competitors have similar approaches, you must be able to help the prospect clearly see the difference *and* clearly see that yours is the best.

Chapter 13

Closing

In sales, much as in life, you get what you ask for. Those who are comfortable asking for more, tend to get more. And those who wait for the customer to close themselves or wait for deals to close on their own, tend to do a lot more waiting than deal closing. One of the best things you can do for yourself is to get extremely comfortable asking for more, more often. Regardless of where you are on the closing spectrum of shy to bold, expanding your comfort zone in this area will substantially increase your sales.

So how does one go from fearful to fearless? It starts with a small shift in perspective. Once we look at this one thing differently, everything else will change. What is this one small shift? It's realizing that our close is simply an offer to help the *prospect*, not ourselves. The numbers game mentality that we've been programmed with taught us that if we close enough prospects we'll eventually get a sale. That each NO was one step closer to a YES. So, we go through as many prospects as need be until we get the sale we're looking for. Then, start that madness all over again. With that mindset, prospects are treated like objects. They are just being used to get a sale. If that description makes the relationship sound cheap to you, it is. And if that's what it sounds like, you can imagine how the prospect *feels* when they are treated that way by people who have that mindset. When we follow the process described in this book, it completely removes us from the equation because it's not about us at all.

Earlier we highlighted the doctor-patient or teacher-student relationship happening in every sales conversation. We're the doctor, not just from an authority standpoint, but also making a recommendation after a diagnosis, which is exactly what the prospect asked for. The only reason they've spent all this time spilling their heart out to you about their problems, is so that you can recommend the best way to fix it. They're not here for a free therapy session or because they're looking to make new friends. They've invested this much time in you for you to deliver in this very moment. Don't let them down.

That perspective may seem convenient and self-serving, but if you think about it, this process gives you the right to have that perspective since you've spent the entire conversation focused on your prospect: *Their* needs, *their* challenges, solutions to *their* problems, and how *their* world will look in the future. On the other hand, if you were to use the numbers game approach having conversations all about you or your product, going from prospect to prospect, firing off pitch after pitch just so you can find someone who will 'give you a sale' you'd be deluding yourself to believe that you're helping anyone but yourself with your close. But since you're *only* taking on clients that are a perfect fit and you can in fact help them tremendously, you owe those prospects the better future you just promised them. And the only way you can fulfill that promise is by closing the deal. So, let's close!

Closing Methods

An entire book could be dedicated to all the different ways to close. In fact, many great books have already been devoted to the topic, but we don't need to spend too much time on that here. Not that it's not important, but if you've followed the process outlined up until this point, then a big close isn't needed. Based on the conversation you just had, the close is just a logical conclusion. It's conversational and feels effortless. Traditional methods of selling rely heavily on the close because the presentation isn't compelling enough. And when you have to rely on a close to compensate for a terrible sales process, the close feels forced. It also feels like a lot of pressure on the receiving end. If sales is a process of creating and managing feelings in our prospects, this is obviously not the feeling we're trying to create. Pressure is good as long as the prospect is creating their own internal pressure. And that's exactly what this process does. But having to resort to external pressure demonstrates weakness and violates the trust that you established with your prospect.

The power behind this process is that every component builds on previous components. So, by the time you get to the close, the prospect is just about ready to go. They don't need much of a push. Let's look at the milestones we've reached by the time we get to the close:

- The prospect acknowledged they have a problem.
- They described all the terrible repercussions that will happen if they don't take care of it.
- They told you that they want to take care of it *now*.
- They described exactly what they want.
- You offered exactly that.
- And you proved you can deliver.

What's left to talk about?! It's time to close the deal and make it official.

There are a few different approaches to closing that I'd like to cover. You can use them independently or combine them to create a close that suits your presentation best.

Recommendation/Suggestion Close: Coming from a place of authority, you're giving your professional opinion on what they should do next. *"Based on everything you told me and everything we discussed, I recommend..."*. The word *recommend* could also be substituted with the word *suggest*. *"I suggest we start with X, and then..."*. What's great about this type of close is that you are the guiding them. You are the driver and they are the passenger. Throughout this entire process you've demonstrated that you are the subject matter expert and you continue to maintain that position of power until the very end, whether they choose to take your advice or not.

Direct Ask: Simply, any question to get the confirmation to move forward. This could be used in conjunction with the recommendation where you ask, *"Would that work for you?"* Or this can be a stand-alone question like, *"Are you ready to get started working together?"*

Alternative Close: This gives the prospect a choice between two options, where either option is an agreement to do business. You can go as far as three options, but my personal favorite is to limit the options to two because the more options the prospect must weigh, the longer it will take them to decide. We would like a decision to be made now. An example of the alternative close would be: *"With the consulting package you get XYZ and it costs $$$, which also includes one-on-one training. With the coaching option you get ABC for $$, and that's more in a group setting. Which of these sounds more appealing to you?"*

People have used and abused the traditional alternative close with silly phrases like, "Would you prefer we start Monday morning or Wednesday afternoon?" Your prospect knows what that is. They know you're not sincerely trying to figure out what day to get started because the day of the week is insignificant compared to the decision to move forward or not. Saying things like, "Would you like to get started with 2 units or 4 units?" is just insulting their intelligence. If you are going to use the alternative close, give legitimate options with clear differences. If the difference in the options you present would significantly impact the future of the relationship, then this won't feel like a close. It will feel like important information that must be discussed as you and your new client are cementing their future together.

Assumptive Close: With the assumptive close, you are just assuming that you and your prospect will be doing business together and you start outlining the next steps. Assumptive closes are powerful because you are eliminating that awkward YES/NO question. Instead of having to ask for permission, you're simply moving forward and asking for forgiveness if you assumed wrong. It's a smooth and easy transition from prospect to client but should only be used when it's appropriate. So, you ask, when is it appropriate? When that assumption is justified. When the client gave you a big enough indication of interest that would allow you to reasonably assume you'll be working together. To assume otherwise is ignorant, condescending, and feels salesy. But if a prospect were to ask you a buying question such as, "How long will it take us to get to the execution stage?" You're answering that question by assuming they're hiring you, and therefore you can continue the conversation with the assumption that they are moving forward.

This sales methodology will allow you to justifiably use the assumptive close more often, simply because it's designed to rapidly move the prospect through each stage of their buying journey. Since you've established trust, given them exactly what they asked for, and proved that you can deliver, their questions tend to be high-quality questions about specific details they need to accurately depict how things will work in the future. Whereas, traditional sales processes are missing key pieces of information, causing the prospect to get stuck in their journey and ultimately forcing them to ask terrible questions that never allow you to assume anything.

Standardizing Your Close

Without consistency, there can be no predictability. Our goal is to standardize our process so that we can deliver the same performance repeatedly and know what to expect from these actions. Through this repetition, skill skyrockets, and so do the number of clients that you convert. We standardize our entire process by standardizing each component individually, which is why you want to come up with one close that you use every time. The more often you say it, the smoother it will sound, and the more confident you will be closing. Closing is all about delivering confidence. With a confident close, you are *demonstrating* that what you are asking for is not only appropriate, but it is expected. And you'll find that prospects live up to the expectations you set, consciously or unconsciously.

The Magic of Urgency

Our goal is for the prospect to decide, right here and now, whether they want to do business with us or not. In fact, the act of making the decision is more important to us than the decision itself. Why? Because the Law of Diminishing Interests states that the longer your prospect takes to act, the less likely they are to do it. Right in this moment we have the highest probability of the decision going our way. We just helped them create the ultimate cocktail of both pain and pleasure, and we want them to decide while all the information is fresh in their mind. Unless they took great notes, as time goes on only a small portion of your conversation will be remembered. And how can they make an educated decision without all the facts, right?

Truth is, we're more concerned about the emotions that dissipate than we are about facts not being remembered. If there's something we don't want them to forget, it's how scary their fear is and how exciting their future feels with you in it, solving all their problems. When the decision is put off to the future, you risk your prospect losing the emotional charge you've just created. Which really means, less conversions, longer sales cycles, more haggling on price, you know, all the things you've had to deal with in the past.

Obviously, some decisions can't be forced. You can't expect to deal with a huge enterprise and expect a big decision to be made in a day or even by one person. But you can look to incorporate urgency every opportunity you have at each step of the way, even if it's with only one person at a time. The point is that if there is no urgency, deals stall. Urgency is a powerful motivator because we tend to put things that are urgent above all, even in front of things that are more important. The urgency *makes* it important because it's important right now. Urgency will create the momentum you need to move deals forward faster.

Proposals – The Deal Killer

Sending proposals is a common practice in many industries and, in my opinion, often unnecessary. Sometimes we send them because we were taught that is what we are supposed to do.

So, just like many bad practices that have been taught to us, we incorporate it into our sales process and add an unnecessary step that will kill some deals. Other times we send them because the prospect asks for a proposal, since they too were taught that is the protocol. But remember, we're leading this relationship and we're driving this sales meeting. They are not nearly as experienced in buying our service as we are in selling it. And since they're knowledge is limited, it's our responsibility to guide the prospect through the buying process. We educate them on how a decision like this is made and when it's made. Sending a proposal in lieu of getting a commitment right in that moment, is not the best course of action since it won't help either party. It just makes it more likely that the buyer will move on with their problem unsolved and the seller move on without a client that would have been a perfect fit.

There are 3 main reasons proposals kill our deals:

Time Kills all Deals: You heard that time heals all wounds? It can also kill all deals. Our goal is to get the prospect to make the decision while those emotional drivers we created, are driving the prospect to a YES. Sending a proposal tells the prospect that the decision doesn't have to be made in this moment, it's the opposite of urgency. The time that we give them to look through the proposal and evaluate options, reduces the probability of closing the deal. The Law of Diminishing Interest is working against us, cooling the prospect off more and more with each passing hour.

Remember what we said earlier. When we feel pain we either fix the problem or find a way to feel better about it. As time goes on, the pain doesn't feel as bad. This makes us think that we don't really need to do anything about our problem because it doesn't seem like much of a problem at all. And it doesn't just stop with the pain, the pleasure wears off as well. As time goes on things just don't seem as exciting as they once sounded. This is the exact opposite of everything we created through the process.

Consistency but no Commitment: Sending a proposal is typically done through email, which means your prospect responding to your proposal will also be done via email. The problem is that it's much easier to reject someone over email than it would be to do it over the telephone or face to face (and in that order too). Since it's easier to say NO, as you might expect, NO happens more often. But when there's rapport and you're having a live conversation, it's much harder for your prospect to reject you. People tend to just go with the flow. That 'flow' that they're going with is simply an expectation that has been set during the conversation. And when that expectation has been set, there's an internal pressure, almost an obligation, to 'do the right thing' in these moments.

According to Robert Cialdini's Principle of Consistency and Commitment, people have a general desire to appear consistent in their behavior, and they value that same consistency in others. If throughout the entire conversation the prospect had talked about moving in the direction of fixing their problem, taking any action otherwise would be inconsistent and perceived as negative. Since an act like that may break rapport and have other unfavorable social consequences, an internal pressure is created within your prospect to ensure that their actions remain consistent with their words. By choosing to send a proposal instead of asking for a commitment, you are choosing to neglect one of the most powerful principles of influence.

The Hardest Objection to Overcome is the One You Don't Hear: If your prospect doesn't want to commit or has a concern, when would be a good time to hear about it, now or later down the line? Now, of course. Your prospect may have some preconceived notions or made some assumptions that are stopping them from moving forward. We'd like to get those things out in the open and clear them up, so they can get passed whatever it is that's holding them back. But as time goes on, uncovering the root issue becomes a harder task because what we lose over time is honesty.

Imagine this, you've just given your presentation and demonstrated the full value of what you bring to the table in the relationship. As their trusted advisor, rapport and trust are at an all-time high. If there are any reservations on the prospect's side, now would be the time to get to the root of what's holding them back, so you can help them get passed it. But sending a proposal before getting a verbal commitment often inhibits you from hearing those reservations. You've seen this scenario: everything seems fine and dandy, with indications of interest and buying signals left and right. You thought the call went great, assumed those buying signals meant that they were going forward, and you sent a proposal- only to find out the following week that they're going to hold off for now. And that's if you even get them on the phone.

If there's anything preventing us from moving forward, we want to know right now so we don't waste any time getting to the bottom of it. In this moment, they'll be most honest with us since trust and rapport are at their peak. The longer we wait, the less likely the objections we hear will be at the true core of what's holding them back. In the next chapter we'll get into why this happens but for now just remember, the hardest objection to overcome is the one you never heard.

What if Proposals are Necessary?

You may be reading this in an industry where proposals are a staple to doing business, and that's okay. The issue I have isn't the proposal itself, it's the idea of you wasting your valuable time, putting together a proposal for someone who doesn't even know if they want to do business with you. They don't mind having you jump through hoops, having you spend hours putting together 4 different options and calling your clients to ask permission to give out their name as a reference, all while the prospect talks to 3 other companies just like you, wasting everyone's time. You should respect your time and the value you bring, enough to say that you'll gladly do all that work as long as they are committed to moving forward. Relationships should be 50/50 or nothing.

A simple solution to all of this is just to talk through a verbal version of the proposal before going through all the work of creating one. As we discussed, wasting time is not the only issue. We know that if we discuss options and ask for a commitment, that gives us the highest probability of converting the prospect to a client. We also know by sending a proposal, so they can review options, we're not asking for a commitment until a follow up conversation, where the prospect doesn't have the same emotional juice they have today. Technically we'd want to walk them through a proposal anyway so that we can interpret the information properly and address any concerns they have immediately, so why wait for a follow up conversation to do that? Why not just go through options now to help them determine the most appropriate option for their situation, and ask to move forward? Your closing ratio will skyrocket if you do.

Clients will respect you more when you take control and show that you value your time. It builds trust because you are demonstrating that you deserve the lead position in the relationship you are asking for. An example would be something like, *"John, I'll absolutely send you a proposal, but let's make sure we interested in doing business together first."* If someone were to ask you to create a proposal with multiple options, I'd say something like, *"I can put something together for you. At the same time, I don't want to waste your time or mine with options that don't make sense for you, so let's talk through them now."* If you come to an agreement and the prospect wants to move forward, then write it up. The proposal is just a formality. It's used more as the written agreement than a formal proposal of options.

Sometimes I'm asked how this would work when there are multiple decision-makers in the company. The answer to that is simply, we apply this approach every opportunity we can and when it comes to the ones we can't, we just have to accept that our chances of winning the sale become significantly lower. As a general practice, do everything in your power to get all the decision-makers in the meeting, so this doesn't become an issue. At times it's not possible but, you'd be surprised at how often it really is possible. Over time you'll get more and more comfortable making demands and operating from a position of power. When you know that you have the ability to generate new clients as often as you need, you'll no longer operate from fear. Fear limits your opportunities. This confidence will open doors for you that are not opened for others. Remember, in sales you only get what you ask for. Ask for more.

Offer an Incentive to Decide Now

Our goal when closing is to bring the sales conversation to a conclusion, a *close*. Whether the status in your CRM lists this prospect as Closed Won or Closed Lost, the goal is to get it closed. Not only because we know this is the best time to get the prospect to decide, but also because the faster this is closed, the faster you can move on to the next opportunity. When your 'Deals Won' are closed faster it means shorter sales cycles, and more sales in a 12-month period. When your 'Deals Lost' are closed faster it means more opportunities in a 12-month period, which also means more sales in that timeframe. The longer it takes your prospects to decide, the more it costs you in both time and opportunity, and the less money you make.

For all these reasons, we want to incentivize our potential new client to make the decision faster. We don't have to force them to do it using external pressure, we can bribe them with an offer which creates internal pressure for them to decide now. This can be special pricing or some added value that they can only get if they agree to move forward today. It's important that whatever this incentive is, it must never be available anytime else in the future. For example, at MindStorm sometimes we'll offer a 'Action-Taker Bonus' where they will get special pricing if we have a signed agreement within 24 hours.

Sometimes the bonus has nothing to do with pricing at all. For example, we have proprietary software that we've developed based on our prospecting methodology. We don't sell the software as a standalone product and, at times, the only way to get this technology is to unlock the bonus. Your bonus can be many things, such as, additional services, other people's products that you exclusively have access to, or anything of value. Your goal is to make your incentive so compelling that they must decide one way or the other, right now.

I'll exaggerate for a moment to make my point. Imagine that the business that you are proposing doing together has a contract value of $15,000. If you were to do something outrageous like offer a $5,000 credit if they were to sign the contract today, that would be hard to ignore. It would be so compelling in fact, that if they don't do it today at $10,000 then they probably won't do it next week for $15,000, which actually means, it's now or never. Your incentive doesn't have to be that dramatic, but the exaggerated example shows that if the incentive is big enough, it can compel your prospect to make the decision now.

Incentive Integrity

Operating from integrity is vital to your success because in business, trust is the number one asset you have. Without it, business would be impossible. So, it should be no surprise that when it comes to your incentive, integrity is just as important. It's crucial that you stick to whatever rules you set for the incentive and don't violate those rules under any circumstances even if it costs you a sale. For example, we had someone come back to us after the 24 hours and say they're ready to move forward but they wanted the special pricing. You can imagine how hard it is to have tell a prospect that you can't give them the incentive because they missed the deadline by a day, knowing full well that it's going to piss them off and most likely kill the deal. It's easy to justify extending the offer and telling ourselves that the deadline could have just as easily been a 48-hour one instead of the 24. That is true. But what is also true is that we didn't choose a 48-hour deadline. We chose to give a bonus if the contract came in within 24 hours, and it did not.

The point is that there should be no gray area. As you can imagine, that prospect was initially frustrated they couldn't get the special pricing. But would they really want to work with a company that *would* give it to them? That would be so much worse. We're not selling used cars here. Telling someone that they will only get a discount if they meet a deadline, and then giving it to them anyway when that deadline is missed, means there was no real deadline. It means you'll say anything to get what you want. It reminds me of the joke where the doctor gives the patient 6 months to live, but when the patient can't pay his bills, the doctor gives him another 6 months. Your incentive is either real or it's not. The fact that your bonus disappears is the very thing that makes it so attractive and valuable. If you're willing to give that bonus at any time, that's not an incentive, that's the standard price.

Reduce the Risk

There's a thin line between excitement and fear. It's a very similar energy, just one is positive and the other is negative. Since nobody wants to get their hopes up, the more excited we get about something, the more fearful we can become of being let down. A cocktail of fear and excitement is anxiety. It's like having one foot on the brake while the other flooring the gas pedal; spinning our wheels, burning ourselves out as we bounce back and forth between excitement and fear, yet not moving anywhere. A prospect in this state is not buying. For them to move down the Speed Path, we must get them to release the brake by eliminating the fear they have, of you not being able to make good on your promise.

There are many ways to deliver the pieces of information they need to release the brake, and I call these validation tools. Some examples are: case studies, testimonials, references, user reviews, statistics, peer reviewed studies, and third-party audits. They all demonstrate that what you are saying is true and you can deliver the outcome the prospect is looking for. You can offer these validation tools before, during, and after your presentation. These can come in many formats: before and after pictures, written or video testimonials, screen shots, reports, etc. The more you have in your arsenal, the higher the probability of you closing the deal.

People want the benefit you're offering but don't want to take a risk, hence the gas/brake. Offering the benefit while simultaneously reducing or eliminating the risk makes the difference between *interest* and *purchase*. It's your responsibility to *prove* beyond a shadow of a doubt that you can deliver the destination you are dangling in front of them.

Another way to reduce the risk is to eliminate it completely. Not all businesses can offer a money back guarantee, but if you can, it makes a big difference. From the prospect's perspective, "Why do I have to take all the risk? If the company is so confident, why aren't they willing to share the risk?" Most business owners that are in the service business are scared to death when I bring up guaranteeing their work. Their fear is that they end up doing work and for whatever reason, not get paid for it. Imagine how the prospect feels. They have no idea if you can deliver. If it's scary for you to put a money back guarantee, then it's scarier for them. If you're worried about the 'what ifs', trust me they are too. A simple solution to this would be to guarantee an outcome you *can* guarantee. Regardless of how small or seemingly insignificant it is, commit to an outcome and deliver it. Allow your relationship to move in smaller steps if you must because that first piece of business should have little or no risk to the prospect.

> **Side Note:** Once you have a guarantee, make sure you use it. It's such a powerful sales tool and you'd be surprised how many people leave it out of their presentations or only bring it up when a prospect asks. We're driving, not our prospects. We never want to hope they ask the right questions for us to deliver the best presentation possible. Bring up your guarantee in every single presentation you give.

Lower the Barrier to Entry

The easier it is to do business with us, the more business we'll have. Therefore, to generate to the highest number of clients, our goal is to make it as easy to do business with us as possible. I was talking with a new client the other day and he said that he was amazed at our sales process. He was comparing his experience as a prospect to what they do at their company and saw many of the things they do wrong. Although I can't share too much information because of strict NDAs that we sign, I will share some of the main differences between our offering and his:

His Offering:

- **Contract Term:** Annual
- **Cost Focus:** Total Contract Value
- **Guarantee:** None

Our Offering:

- **Contract Term:** Month to Month (after 90 day minimum)
- **Cost Focus:** Monthly Rate
- **Guarantee:** 100% Money Back

Without knowing his industry or hearing one word of any sales presentation, if you were a prospect, which deal seems more appealing to you? It's the one that's easier to digest. Your prospect is always weighing risk vs reward, which means, your goal is to always figure out how to make your deal less risky and more rewarding for your prospect. Since he was comparing how we structured our offering versus his, let's compare the two, point by point. For reference, we'll call my client Eric.

Contract Term: Eric was asking his prospects to commit to a year. Unheard of? No. But we were only asking for a 90-day commitment. If someone has never done business with you, it will take a lot of reassurance to make them feel comfortable locking into a year-long contract. Even if you have a big brand name and the best product or service in the market, the "I can't change my mind for a whole year?" is scary. So now if you're Eric, you may have the best product in the market but since you don't have a big brand name to fall back on, you still must prove that you can deliver. Which means there are two things going against you, you must prove to your prospects you can deliver, *and* you'd have to make them feel better about the fact that they can't change their mind for another 12 months.

What all prospects fear is, "What if I'm wrong?" Often, being wrong is worse than the money lost by being wrong. We all have a fear of failure. That fear can paralyze us, make us second-guess our decisions, and ensure we have every escape route possible so we can exit a bad situation with the least amount of damage. A lengthy contract says to your prospect, "I'm not allowing you to have an escape route, but I do want you to trust me." That's hard to do because those two things feel like they conflict, at least when you've never done business with this person. When Eric asked me if he would be required to sign a long-term contract, my answer was, "We can work month to month. I only want you to work with us for as long as you find it valuable. If at any time you want to stop, we stop."

> **Side Note:** It may not make sense for your business to allow clients the opportunity to come and go as they please. By no means am I suggesting that long-term contracts are a bad thing. In fact, for one client we helped create and implement a '5-year Price Lock Guarantee.' Was it a 5-year contract? Yes, but it didn't feel like one. See, for that client we made it

very clear to their customers that they were signing a long-term contract, but we invested the time training on how to deliver the message in a way where that was a good thing, not a bad thing. Their customers felt the longer the term the better because a long-term relationship is exactly what they're looking for and they were promised that prices would never go higher, regardless of the crazy price increases of raw material that market experiences at times. The point is, it's all about how your offering is packaged. It can be packaged in a way where it feels like a big hurdle to get over or it can be packaged in a way that allows for a very easy decision to be made. Let's go back to Eric and I'll explain more of what I mean.

Guarantee: Although he was asking his prospects for this long contract term, Eric felt he couldn't offer any guarantee because there was a certain level of work needed to be completed by the client. He was afraid that if he did his part, but the client didn't do theirs, he would be at risk. When I asked how many times in the last 17 years of business that he hadn't produced the results promised, whether it was his fault or his clients, his answer was zero! That math alone tells me to take the risk and eat the loss if a client got in the way of results because in the last 17 years there had to be clients of his that didn't do what they were supposed to, and he was still able to deliver. But to Eric's defense, the value of a one-year contract can be as high as $1,000,000. A full guarantee would be impossible, irresponsible, and more like an insurance policy.

My recommendation to Eric was just guarantee a portion of it. If he can guarantee the first part of the relationship, his performance would give the client the confidence to continue. For example, I offered a money-back guarantee on the first three months of my relationship with Eric, based on our first project which was lead generation. Eric and his sales team had been struggling to generate leads and secure meetings with high-level executives at target companies. They've tried cold calling, direct mail campaigns, and email campaigns, even sent baskets of cookies to executives. But nothing worked.

I knew we could help him. Since the relationship would be brand new, I offered a guarantee in writing that the outbound system we would build for his team would generate leads and secure telephone meetings with high level executives, or he could have his money back. The only condition was that he would give us 90 days to build, implement, and train our methodology. We wouldn't be able to guarantee something that wasn't completed. After the 90 days, it would be month to month as promised. At that moment, Eric had a choice of what was more important to him, the ability to leave before 90 days or the guarantee that he would get what he wanted, or it would cost him nothing. Eric chose the guarantee.

What's great for Eric was that in his first two weeks he generated 10 appointments with high level executives using our LinkedIn methodology, and he was very happy. Although I knew all along that he'd get those results, he was hopeful at best. What a better way to reassure him than to completely remove the risk for him? And now that this experience demonstrated that we deliver what we promise, it gives him ability to continue the relationship without me having to guarantee every step of the way.

This is an important example because consultants rarely guarantee *anything*. We can only advise, and the client must take that advice and apply it. But we still *found* a way to make it work, which means so can you. Think about what outcome you can guarantee and focus on that. For us, it required more work. It required more time training Eric and his team, and it also required us to be more hands-on to ensure campaigns were launched when and how we advised. But it was completely worth it. Think about what you can do to guarantee more in the beginning of your relationship so that you make it easier for your client to buy.

Cost Focus: The final point I'll make comparing Eric's process to ours, is the focus on cost. Which of these feels like the bigger decision, $5500 a month or $66,000 a year? The bigger the number, the bigger the decision. The bigger the decision, the longer it takes to make, and the less frequently we'll hear a YES. It's the same reason Sally Struthers would ask people to donate "Just 70 cents a day" to her charity. When it's broken down so small it seems insignificant. Think about your offering and how you frame it. What are you focusing on? What decision are you asking your prospect to make? Does it seem big and scary? Or does it seem small and insignificant? The lower the barrier to entry, the more deals you'll close.

This may mean, structuring your deal differently by breaking it into smaller steps so that it's easy to take that first step. Research shows existing customers are, by average, 6 times more likely to purchase from you when compared to a new prospect. The only difference between a prospect and customer is one transaction. Which means, you can lower your initial offering to establish that very significant, first transaction. This will not only get more clients in the door, but once their status changes from prospect to client, you can upsell them into something more. There's no point in trying to do two steps in one. The client moving from the first step to the next doesn't feel like it's that big of a jump, especially since they are 6 times more likely to say YES to that second step now that a relationship has been established.

We all want to close big deals. But why risk not getting any deal done simply to satisfy our ego? We lower the barrier to entry because it's not about that first piece of business. Our goal isn't to win the sale, it's to win the relationship. If we make it about the sale, our sales will be much lower overall. But if we're focused on systematically generating and maximizing relationships, sales will skyrocket.

When building a structured sales process, it's important that you are strategic in everything you do. You are not looking to operate on a whim and vary your approach with each sales conversation. You want a process that is followed every time. A system that gives you the highest likelihood of converting prospects to clients, and then develops each of those relationships to maximize both the value you deliver and the revenue you generate. This means, you methodically plan every offer at every stage. You have the same go-to close that you deliver every time. If you get a YES, then you eventually upsell your new client to a higher priced offering that delivers even more value. If you get a NO on your initial offer, you down sell to a smaller offering. Have your strategic process mapped out so that no matter where your prospect goes, you can respond with the best course of action, at the most appropriate time.

In Closing (See what I did there?)

What's most important about closing is that it gives direction. It's a call to action, telling people what they'll have to do next to benefit from all the great information they've just heard. Without it, it was just information. A perfect example of this happened when I was at an event listening to a speaker talk about how to change our internal wiring so that we can get past our own limitations. This is one of my favorite personal improvement topics and since I've invested a lot of time learning this subject, I was surprised that 'Paul' was delivering information that I haven't heard before, a new perspective to some material that's been passed around.

When Paul's time on stage ran out, he thanked us all and said his goodbyes. As I was reading the sheet he handed out, I noticed that he was only able to get through a little more than half of the material he had planned for that afternoon. I couldn't help but wonder what it was we missed. If what I found was so valuable, what other tricks up his sleeve did he plan on sharing with us? Moreover, what other insight or training does he provide in general? Surely, he had much more content than the material he planned to deliver in just one afternoon.

Although my mind was racing, the next speaker came on and changed our focus. I went back to my hotel that evening and looked at Paul's website. I planned to purchase some of his courses, but I figured I'd go through them when I was recharged the next day. As you can imagine, I never did. I got busy, life got in the way, and he and his material was forgotten until this moment almost a year later. I'll look into again now that I'm focused on it, but even if he gets a sale from me now, wouldn't he have liked to have that a year ago? And if I had purchased last year, who knows how much business I would have done with him by now.

Paul gave a lot of great information but what was his sales strategy? Did he think that people were going to say, "I'd love to work with that guy one-on-one to take my business to the next level. Let me call him"? That's not how it works. For the record, I put this book on hold to reach out to a few others that I connected with at the seminar, asking each one if they'd purchased anything from Paul, since they all loved his session. The answer was no on all counts. In fact, when I initially described who I was talking about, most had a similar response, "Oh yeah, what was his name?" And, as much as they all said they would like to see what courses he sells and hear him speak at another event when we were at the seminar, I was the only one that went as far as even visiting his website.

All Paul would have needed to do to get a completely different outcome was to say, "I had a lot more material to share that I know you'll love but unfortunately we ran out of time, so for those of you who would like to discuss how you can get more of these strategies, you can follow me to the back." What Paul had done is similar to what a lot of salespeople do. They deliver great information but rely on the prospect to take the next step without any direction. If we don't give instruction on what the prospect needs to do next, something or someone else will distract them, just as the next speaker did with our group. Paul became 'this guy that we heard at this seminar once' instead of getting new clients that were in that room. Don't assume your prospect will take the next step on their own, hold their hand and walk them through it. Give direction and get a commitment at the most opportune time, right there on the spot.

Chapter 14

Overcoming Objections

Dealing with objections is rarely viewed as a positive experience. Most would say it's their least favorite part of the sales process. Some cringe at even the slightest sound of resistance coming from their prospect, simply because they associate any type of opposition with not getting the sale. We get so conditioned to believe that NO is bad, and YES is good, but the truth is neither of those mean anything. Non-buyers are often in agreement with you along the way, until the end when it counts, which means, all those YESes you had gotten meant nothing. Conversely, if you look back to most of your sales, they actually have come from people who had given you some type of objection, which means, all those NOs you received meant nothing as well.

My goal is to completely change your perspective on objections, because once you realize that they're actually a great thing you'll greet them differently when faced with them. Let's start with the realization that only a small percentage of prospects roll over and buy without any questions or having any concerns along the way. Most of your interactions will require you to deal with prospects that may have been misinformed, or have made false assumptions. Part of your responsibility is to educate buyers, give them different points of view, and alleviate their fears. Understanding this, objections aren't just part of the process, they are the process. They're on the very path that leads to a sale, the Speed Path.

Ryan Holiday, author of one of my favorite books, *The Obstacle Is the Way*, says it best: *"The obstacle in the path becomes the path. Never forget, within every obstacle is an opportunity to improve our condition."* That opportunity, in this context, is that the objection will tell us exactly what we need to do to close the sale. It points directly to the problem that is getting in the way of a transaction happening and a relationship forming. Without knowing what that is, how do we address it? If we can't address it, how will that problem ever get solved, or the prospect get past it? They probably won't.

Think about how hard sales would be if we didn't get objections. Could you imagine our prospects staying silent or refusing to tell us why they don't want to do business with us? Objections are a blessing, because once we know the formula for interpreting that information, it's like the buyer giving us verbal instructions on how to close the deal. Let's look at what that formula is.

Only 3 Objections

How much easier would sales be if there were only three objections to overcome? Instead, it seems like prospects have an infinite supply of ways to object to our recommendation. Years ago, I'd tell salespeople to write a well-thought-out response to the top five or six objections they get most often. Not only do I believe in being prepared, but since you can't possibly prepare for an unlimited number of potential responses, this follows the 80/20 rule where you can focus on the top twenty percent of the objections that you would get 80 percent of the time.

As my focus shifted from the salesperson to the prospect, everything changed. It became about what the prospect needed to move forward, not about what the salesperson needed to get past it, and certainly not about coming up with clever responses. I realized that if I could identify what each objection really meant, then we could always respond with the best course of action by giving the prospect what they needed to make a purchase. I started writing down every objection I could think of. As I went through the list, I couldn't believe what I was seeing.

First, I realized this was a problem-solution situation. The prospect has a problem with moving forward and the only way forward was to provide a solution to that problem. Since my whole sales approach was based on problem-solution, why would my approach to objections be any different? We'll cover this in a minute. As I started listing solutions to each problem (objection), I noticed that regardless of what crazy objection someone can throw at you, there were only 3 buckets they can fit in to: No Trust, No Resources, or No Motivation. Sometimes the objection fits in only one bucket and other times it's a combination of multiple buckets because they have multiple issues. By determining which bucket the objection is in, we'll know what we must deliver to move the relationship forward. Any other response will not be effective.

No Trust: When it comes to any relationship, trust is the foundation. Without it, people won't take risks and the relationship will never fully develop. This is true whether in personal or business relationships. You wouldn't risk telling a secret to someone you didn't trust, banks don't risk lending money to those they don't trust, and people don't buy from salespeople or companies they don't trust. Although there are always exceptions, we can say that as a general rule, that statement is true.

In the bank example, they can quantify their trust with factors like credit score and income, and doing business is determined by risk versus reward, which is also how your prospect decides if they should do business with you. The challenge is that you cannot see your 'trust score.' There's no easy way to quantify the level of trust you are creating during your sales conversations, but I promise you that the total amount of business you do is determined by that imaginary number.

We already know that trust relies on intentions and capability. This trust must be instilled in a variety of areas and in multiple forms. Your prospect must trust:

- You (Intentions & Capability)
- Your Company (Intentions & Capability)
- Your Product, Service, or Offering (Capability)
- Themselves (Capability)

You can see why trust is so important. There are so many ways to doubt getting the outcome you are promising. Unfortunately, trust is a chain that is only as strong as its weakest link. Lack of confidence in any of these areas is enough to kill a deal. The objections you hear are things like:

- I need to speak with my CPA.
- I saw bad reviews online.
- My industry is different.
- I don't know that it will work for me.

If someone needs to get a second opinion from someone else, they don't have enough confidence in yours. In fact, confidence is what's needed in all trust-based objections because if you follow all these objections down to their root cause, it will lead you to your prospect's fear. When I say overcoming objections, what

I'm really suggesting is to help your prospect overcome their *fear*. Again, this is a completely different shift in mindset because sales gurus have always described overcoming objections as something we must *do*, as if we are sparring with the prospect. I imagine that to look like a prospect throwing everything they have at us to protect themselves from buying, while we 'overcome' these attacks and counter with our own verbal Ninjutsu. That is clearly not the most effective approach.

The reality is that overcoming fear is something *they* must do and the only thing we can do is try to help them in their effort. It's important that we do all that we can because their fear, that we can't deliver on our promise, triggers a fear that they're making a bad decision. In turn, that triggers fear that their bad decision will eventually lead to some type of loss: loss of time, loss of money, loss of dignity, wasted effort, or all the above. Our call to action when we hear trust-based objections is to immediately stop this destructive domino effect by delivering the 3 C's: Confidence, Comfort, and Certainty. We remove as much of the risk in the transaction as possible and provide new information that *proves* their fear is not valid. If you are leading from a place of confidence and certainty, all that's left is to comfort and reassure them.

No Motivation: We discussed how all human behavior is shaped by two forces, our need to avoid pain and our desire to gain pleasure. If we get objections that fall into this bucket, it's simply because we didn't establish a big enough *need* (pain) or create a strong enough *desire* (pleasure). How can we expect our prospect to continue down the Speed Path if there's no gas in the tank? Like trust, we can't quantify how motivated our prospects are. We can't look at a dashboard and see a gauge or a score. The only thing we can do is give our best every time and listen for clues that tell us what areas need to be addressed.

Motivation objections have to do with:

- Need – Problem isn't painful enough.
- Desire – Solution doesn't offer enough pleasure.
- Value – Outcome isn't worth the cost or the risk.

Examples of motivation objections are:

- *"There's too much going on right now."*
- *"I don't have any interest."*
- *"I think it's too expensive."*

If your prospect feels they have too much going on to implement your solution, it might mean they don't feel the problem they have is a high enough priority. Or if the problem *is* pressing enough, it can mean that they don't feel your solution is worth the time and energy required to undertake it. There's a cost associated with everything. That cost can take the form of money, time, or other resources, and your prospect is always managing their costs to some extent. They'll never be able to justify paying more than the *value* you're offering. Your perceived value is your current ceiling. If you'd like your prospect to make a bigger investment, then raise your value so that the ROI is high enough to make it an easy decision on their part.

To increase value, focus on: **Need:** the problem/pain, **Desire:** the solution/pleasure, and the **Destination:** the ultimate outcome. Give them a brief summary of the entire process you already took them through. Remind them about the problem they have, the pain it's causing, what happens in the future if they don't take care of it, your solution and its secret sauce, the pleasure it will create, and ultimately where they will end up by having your solution in place. That may sound like a lot to discuss but you can accomplish this in a few sentences. Just make sure you spend the most time and energy focusing on the specific component they've trivialized, because that's the area that's lowering your value.

No Resources: If your prospect wants your offering but doesn't have the resources needed to make the purchase possible, she simply will not be able to move forward. Therefore, our call to action is to help our prospect find those resources or find a way to get the deal done without them. This may be to structure the deal where they can make payments or offer to work the project around the customer's event calendar, etc. When someone doesn't have resources, resourcefulness is needed. Your role is to find solutions to that problem. The resources you mostly hear about are:

- Time
- Money
- People

In most cases, it's not that they don't have the resources, it's that they *feel* that they don't have the resources, or enough resources to feel comfortable moving forward. This is a completely different problem. For example, if someone said they couldn't afford your services, that has nothing to do with being able to physically get their hands on the money. It's just that they may not have enough money to pay for your services along with everything else they want to spend money on. So it boils down to priorities. Very simply, they don't value your offering high enough to replace something else.

The same thing happens with time. We all have the same 24 hours in a day and we make time for things that are most important to us. If we don't have a problem big enough (urgent) or we don't have a desired outcome that is strong enough (important), then we'll never make time for it until it falls in at least one of those categories. Through this process we've used pain and pleasure to make our offering both urgent and important which will reduce the number of these types of objections. Since we must still prepare for them, let's dig deeper into resource-based objections.

If we look at the diagram below, we can see that we have trust on the left and value/motivation on the right. When we get to the root of resource-based objections, we may find that the real objection may be in one of the other categories. This happens because people often use 'lack of resources' as an excuse for not moving forward when it's really something else. We'll use a process that allows us to find the real objection so that we know the proper way to deal with it.

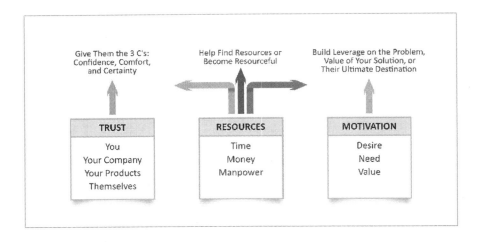

The Phantom Bucket: There's a technical name for objections in this bucket and they're called bullshit objections. Overcoming these objections is a waste of time simply because they are not objections at all. They are merely excuses for not buying. Salespeople fall into this trap by being too eager to respond to any objection they hear. After they give the perfect rebuttal, the prospect hits them with another excuse. This is that battle I described earlier between the salesperson and the prospect, and there's no point in engaging in this because the prospect isn't trying to figure out how to move forward at all. They've already decided that they are not going to make a purchase and they're being dishonest about the reason.

Since we know they have a real objection for not moving forward, but they're choosing to be dishonest about it, what does that tell us? I would want to ask how strong relationships are where people lie to each other. Not very strong at all. The call to action when the prospect isn't being honest would be to re-establish a connection. Their decision to mislead us demonstrates that we are no longer in rapport. They may be worried that if they're honest about their reservations, you'll try to sell them. Or maybe they're embarrassed about the real issue holding them back. Either way, that fear indicates that our relationship isn't as strong as it needs to be for the prospect to move forward. Trust paves the way for the relationship and business can only move as far as trust has been established. Which means the mysterious 4th bucket, isn't really a bucket at all. It's really a trust bucket. We must get back in rapport and get them back to honesty before anything else.

An extension of this issue is when a prospect tells you they don't want to move forward but won't tell you why. You may hear things like, "I'm just not going to do it today" or, "No thanks". If someone doesn't give you an explanation, they simply don't feel like they owe you one. This is a huge red flag because they are basically saying that they don't feel even the slightest bit of obligation to you. They won't even attempt to soften the blow and let you down gently by giving you an excuse. So, if lying in a relationship is bad, this is even worse because it means the prospect doesn't care enough about your feelings to even lie to you!

I bring up the phantom bucket to remind us that knowing how to handle the three different types of objections only helps us when we're dealing with a real objection. Let's walk through a process for cutting through the BS so that we can help our prospect find a way to move forward.

Preemptive Strike

Breaking objections down into three categories, we can see that our sales process preemptively eliminates many of those objections. We establish a strong level of trust in the Connection phase, continue demonstrating trust by acting as their strategic advisor in Discovery, and prove that we can deliver in the Presentation phase. The process puts the prospect at the center of the universe and since it's never about us, they never have to question our intentions.

When it comes to the motivation-based objections, the same thing happens. In fact, this entire methodology was developed to create the highest levels of motivation by harnessing the two forces that drive all human behavior. If this method is followed correctly, then anyone choosing not to move forward based on a motivation-based objection, simply are not the right fit. Not everyone will have a need for your offering and you'll be happy to let these prospects go since you only want those who are perfect for you.

Finally, you'll also hear fewer resource-based objections, since you're now doing a better job targeting and qualifying your prospects. If a prospect doesn't have the budget or the timing isn't right, you wouldn't wait until the end of your sales process to find that out. This method is designed to target the best prospects and convert them to client status with the least amount of time, energy, and effort. It follows Albert Einstein's philosophy, "Everything should be as simple as it can be, but not simpler". By preemptively overcoming most of the objections that would come our way, we eliminate unnecessary, time consuming conversations, so we can invest that time closing more deals.

The Magic Process Repeated

Okay, so the sales methodology outlined in this book isn't exactly magic, but when you follow it, it sure feels like it is. So why not use the same exact influential process to handle our prospect's objections? To do this we follow the first 4 phases of the sales process:

1. **Connect:** Align with the prospect.
2. **Discover:** Ask questions to uncover and isolate the root objection.
3. **Present:** Present new information to solve the problem.
4. **Close:** Ask to move forward.

Connect: When most salespeople hear objections, their typical response is to instantly rebut them. The problem with instantly contradicting your prospect is that it makes your prospect feel like your only concern is to make a sale. You immediately start losing trust.

Even if you had the perfect rebuttal, the fact that you moved so fast to dismiss their concern makes your words seem disingenuous. They don't feel that you really listened to their issue and you had no time to consider the problem they just explained. To them, it means that you demonstrated a lack of empathy by not taking the time to look at things from their point of view. Without connecting, you're asking your prospect to take the time to consider your perspective, even though you're not willing to do the same for them.

To bring your prospect into your world, you must first meet them in theirs. Connecting is simply making a point to acknowledge that they have a difference of opinion, and it demonstrates that you encourage an open dialogue to get to the truth. Since you have nothing to hide, and you are 100% confident that a purchase will better their business and life, you have no problem hearing their point of view, and discussing it further. Of course, the opposite is true too. If you're not willing to do this, it comes off as insecure or you're trying to hide something.

The funny thing is that when I suggest connecting to overcome objections, I'm literally talking about one sentence, or two at the most! How can one sentence imply so much? Let's take a look at connecting in action:

Prospect: *I need time to think about it.*

You: *Of course! It's absolutely key that you're happy with whatever decision you make.*

Did we tell him he was wrong for feeling that way? That this minor decision shouldn't require more time to make? Of course not. We let him know that our interests are aligned. That our primary concern is his wellbeing and what's most important to us is that he's happy with whatever he decides.

Would we like that decision to be made now? Yes. But if we want the ability to weigh in on that decision, then we must first understand what pros and cons he's pondering. We still need to understand what his true objection is and understand why this isn't an obvious YES for him. By connecting first, we take one step back in order to take three forward, because when we do present our perspective, he'll actually listen to what we have to say. By agreeing with him first, we can disagree with him later. Otherwise, he won't listen to any input we give since he'll assume it isn't sincere.

Other Connecting phrases:

- *I appreciate you saying that.*
- *Thank you for bringing that to my attention.*
- *I admire your honesty.*
- *I understand completely.*
- *I know where you're coming from.*
- *It sounds like you're frustrated.*

Salespeople are often scared to connect because they feel that aligning with the prospect will somehow validate the prospect's objection. But you don't have to agree with the prospect to empathize with them. You can acknowledge that they feel a certain way without justifying that it's a reason not to move forward.

Discover: Task (1): Get to the Root Objection- No objection matters other than the one that's stopping your prospect from buying. Therefore, responding to the wrong objection can never move the relationship forward since you're not solving the problem they have. This happens all too often because on the surface, an objection can sound like it belongs in one bucket when really it belongs in another. If the bucket determines how we solve the problem, assuming the wrong bucket means that you deliver an invalid solution. Let's look at an example.

A few years back I went out with a client's sales team to get an idea of what we were going to be working with. I got a chance to spend some time with one of the salespeople, Michael, who'd been with the company for years. Michael was at pains to tell me how he wasn't happy that outside help was coming in, especially because their industry was so different. During the car ride he rattled off all the years of experience he had and how he'd heard every objection under the sun. He was completely convinced that there was no way we would be able to contribute any value to his efforts.

The same way you get the same old objections all the time, so do I. There's always a Michael in the group. But, my goal wasn't to convince him of anything, it was just to evaluate him. He was giving a presentation to a prospect and, at the end, right on cue, asked for the business. The prospect's response was, "I've been with XXX company for more than 6 years now." Michael immediately responded with his go-to rebuttal, going on and on about how business is business and that liking someone personally doesn't justify having to pay more for supplies.

You could physically see the prospect get tense. His face was tightening with every word Michael spoke. I interrupted Michael and said, *"Joe, out of curiosity, what concerns you most about the idea of changing suppliers?"* to which he replied, *"They know me. They're a pain in the ass sometimes but making a switch isn't so simple for me. They know our specific needs, they know what we order. They accommodate our crazy schedule. Their prices are a little higher but it's worth it. I made the mistake of switching once before and it was such a nightmare. It interrupted our business. Everything stopped for 2 days and I'm never taking that chance again."*

Here Michael thought he was getting a motivation objection, where the benefits of the price decrease didn't outweigh the loss of a relationship, but in reality, it was a trust objection. The prospect just didn't want to take the risk of making changes because he didn't have confidence in anyone other than his 'pain-in-the-ass' supplier that he was paying more money to be with. Joe was willing to pay a premium for the peace of mind it gave him. Meanwhile, Michael was telling Joe to ditch a personal relationship he didn't have, for a cost savings that he didn't care about.

When we assume, we lose sales. We want to completely understand what the issue is, *behind* the issue. When someone says, "I don't have the money", does that mean they can't get their hands on it (No Resources) or does that mean they can, but not for your offering (No Motivation)? We'd like to go even further. Assuming they can get their hands on it, would they say YES? Because if the answer is still NO, there's no point helping them find money or restructuring the terms. We need to get to the real issue and resolve *that*.

Getting to the Root Objection:

- *Can you tell me more about that?*
- *What is it about _____ that bothers you most?*
- *Why is that a problem for you?*
- *I'm sure you have a good reason for saying that, would you mind telling me what that is?*
- *How does that affect you most?*
- *What do you fear most about _____?*
- *Why? Or How Come?*
- *Can you expand a little further?*
- *I'd love to hear about that.*
- *Is it _____ or is it really _____?*

The first part of Objection Discovery is getting clarity. We want to ask the magic question, "Why?" as many ways as we can until we understand what the underlying problem is. When we ask questions like these, we get the prospect to open up and share their feelings. Since our goal is to help them change those feelings and overcome some of their limiting beliefs, like a therapist, this is our starting point.

Let's stack some of the principles we've discussed to reiterate a point from earlier. I mentioned that the hardest objection to overcome is the one you never hear. Also, that we must solve the root objection before the prospect will ever agree to move forward. Which means, if we never hear the root objection, we can't overcome it and, therefore, a sale won't happen. So, if many of the objections (if not all) are rooted in some form of fear, what would be required for the prospect to open up to us? Since we need them to be completely honest with us, and allow themselves to be vulnerable, what would be required for that to happen?: a massive amount of interest, trust, and rapport.

If they don't have interest, then there's nothing more to talk about. If there's no trust, then they'll never allow themselves to be vulnerable around you. Sharing their true feelings, especially their fears, simply won't happen. And if there isn't rapport, they don't feel that they owe you any explanation. So, if these three things are vital to getting to the real objection, and that issue is critical to getting the prospect to move forward, then the question is, when do you have the highest levels of interest, trust and rapport? You guessed it, during that window of opportunity we discussed earlier, right after the presentation. This is the reason we absolutely have to ask for a commitment when the presentation is complete. Sending a proposal and following up days later, attempts to engage the prospect when they've gone completely cold. When they tell you NO, any objection you get will be a surface level objection because they're not in the same emotional state you'd helped them get to. But when you take them through this process, they're in a prime state to get to the real issue that's stopping them from moving forward. They're also the most receptive to your suggestion, which makes overcoming objections far more effective.

What I love the most about getting clarity is that it tells us exactly how to solve the problem. Here's an example:

Prospect: *I won't sign a 5-year contract.*

You: *How come? Do you switch vendors often?*

Prospect: *No, I've been with Acme Corp for 9 years. I just don't like contracts.*

You: *I can understand that. Other than the contract, do you have any other issue?*

Prospect: *No. I like everything you described, just not a 5-year contract!*

You: *Out of curiosity, what is it about the agreement that scares you most?*

Prospect: *I may find out that you guys are terrible, and I couldn't risk getting stuck for the next 5 years in a bad situation if you guys don't deliver what you promise.*

You: *Is that your main issue or is there something else?*

Prospect: *That's my main concern.*

If a contract was a requirement, then we can create a win-win situation where he has an 'out' of the contract if we don't fulfill our end of the bargain. This way, he doesn't feel trapped, we get a new customer with a 5-year commitment, and everyone is happy. Without knowing *why* the problem is a problem, we may have never figured out a solution in this scenario - especially when having or not having a contract is a deal-breaker for both sides.

Discover: Task (2): Isolate the Objection- We know that sometimes we hear objections that aren't real. Other times they're real but not the dominant reason the prospect is hesitating. Before we jump into solving the problem, we want to make sure that it's a problem worth solving. In the scenario above we isolated the objection by asking, "Other than the contract, do you have any other issue?" A prospect can have multiple concerns about moving forward, and we want to hear about all of them. Since we can only address one at a time, it's important to tackle the biggest obstacle first: the one that represents the biggest issue for them. Once you get past that one, the next becomes easier for both you and your buyer. Eventually, you'll work your way down the line, systematically dismantling each potential threat, one by one.

And something amazing happens when you isolate an objection. You can then eliminate many other objections that normally arise. Let's assume that the prospect has a major issue and a few minor ones. Normally, you'd work to solve one and then she'd throw others at you. But what if you asked questions like, *"Besides X, are there any other concerns that you have? Or is that the main issue?"* If it's the main issue, she typically responds with, "That's my main issue". If there was something more important to her, she'd respond with something like, "My main concern is ...".

Isolating the objection gets to the core issue and also removes other objections from the conversation, leaving you with just one objection to overcome. And once you definitively solve that problem, you've just converted your prospect to a client. Sounds too easy? Well it is. It's much easier than having to overcome a mountain of objections that are piled on you. To understand why this works so well, let's look at it from the prospect's perspective at the point you're asking these questions.

We'll use the contract example. If your prospect liked most of what you said but he just can't see himself going forward because of a 5-year contract, then there's no need to talk about anything else. The other issues are insignificant in comparison. So, by asking, *"Are there other concerns or is this the main issue?"* you're getting him to choose one problem, the biggest problem, and forgo all others. As he verbally commits to this one issue, he makes a declaration that he will most likely remain consistent with going forward. In other words, because he chose to identify only one problem, chances are he will commit. It will be much harder for him to come up with another one after he declared that he only had one issue.

You can do this with any scenario. Before jumping to solve a problem, just make sure that it's the only one to solve. Some phrases you can use are:

- *Other than _____, what other concerns do you have?*
- *If ____ wasn't an issue for you, would you move forward?*
- *Is it _____ or is it really something else?*
- *Is _____ really the main issue or is there something more important?*

Present- This is the portion of the standard rebuttal that you're used to. This is where we bring new information to the table to either directly fix the problem or make the prospect feel better about it. Fixing the problem is something that you can do, by lowering a price or offering terms, for example. It's a way to accommodate the prospect by offering something he was not previously offered, thereby making the deal more enticing. Here are some examples of actions you can take to 'fix' problems:

Trust:

- Supply references.
- Offer to work on a performance basis.
- Send case studies, testimonials, or proof you can deliver.
- Offer a guarantee.

Resources:

- Lower price/absorb some of the cost.
- Break up payments/offer terms.
- Absorb some of the workload (No time).

Motivation:

- All the above.
- Throw in additional incentives.

Sometimes there's nothing more you can do other than give them a new perspective. And as simple as that sounds, many times that's all that is needed because a new point of view will make them feel better about that situation. For example, a prospect once told me that our fees were high. When I asked, *"Compared to what?"* he realized that he really didn't have a solid reference to form that opinion. My response was, let's figure out together if it makes sense for you or not. After he did the math, he realized he'd been paying salespeople an extraordinary amount of money throughout the years, and they hadn't done much in terms of bringing in sales, not to mention all the marketing costs, insurance costs, travel expenses, and everything else that came with having those people. Once I was able to remind him of the opportunity cost associated with his team not knowing what they were doing, and how much more money he was on track to waste in the next 3 years, my fee was no longer high. Sometimes it's just a matter of putting things in perspective or context.

But would I have had the opportunity to give that perspective if the prospect didn't already like me? Would he have gone through the process of adding up all the costs if he didn't trust me? Of course not. Having a good rebuttal is easy, creating an environment where your prospect feels safe and trusts what you say is harder. They know what's coming. They know that you're going to present a point of view that recommends they make the purchase. What they *don't* know is if you're suggesting that purchase because you want to make a sale or because it's in their best interest. Which means, *how* you deliver your rebuttal is more important than anything you're going to say. My response of, "Let's together figure out if it makes sense for you or not" says that I'm perfectly fine with us concluding that this isn't the best fit for you. That is what builds trust. But again, you can't fake this. You aren't trying to 'close' everyone. You're only looking to help those who *are* a perfect fit, get out of their own way.

Close: Every great presentation should end with a close. This is true whether we're talking about the overall sales process or overcoming objections. This is the call to action that tells the prospect what to do with the new information you gave him. Without the close, your rebuttal is just your point of view. The close is the catalyst that can converts your words to the prospect's actions. Sometimes I hear salespeople give rebuttals without closing. In response, the prospect objects and this goes back and forth three or four times. But since there is no close, the prospect is technically just objecting to their point of view! It looks something like this:

Prospect: *It's outside of our budget.*

Salesperson: *We do have financing options.*

Prospect: *Yeah, but I don't want to take on more debt.*

Salesperson: *If you think about it, the ads you place will help increase sales, so it will pay for itself.*

Prospect: *That's what you say. What happens if I don't? Do I still have to pay you?*

Salesperson: *Only for the ads that ran but you can stop anytime if it's not working for you.*

Prospect: *I just can't afford to take that chance right now. Maybe sometime in the future. Call me in 6 months.*

There are so many things wrong with an exchange like this, but I'll quickly name three. First, the salesperson is only reacting to surface level objections. But it's not actually about the money: the prospect just doesn't want to do it, so getting to that underlying reason is absolutely critical. Second, the prospect is dismissing every one of the salesperson's attempts to solve the problem. Partially because the prospect wasn't being honest about the problem, so the salesperson is giving solutions that mean nothing to the prospect. But also, look how the salesperson never connected on the first objection. We can't expect the prospect to take into consideration the solution we're proposing when we show that we aren't willing to take the time to consider the problem he feels he has. So, from the very first objection, the salesperson and the prospect took turns dismissing each other's point of view.

Third, the salesperson never closed! In that conversation there were three different opportunities to directly ask for the business, where the prospect would have had to say NO three different times, yet it never happened once. Without a close at the end of each point, we're just going back and forth as if we're having some sort of philosophical debate about business. Our goal is to move the deal forward. We do that by taking one objection at a time, making sure we're dealing with the root of the biggest obstacle they see in moving forward, definitively solve that problem, and then put them in a position where they must make a decision. Rinse and repeat.

Let's face it, sometimes your prospect is just being fearful. In this state they're indecisive and don't want to commit to anything. Their objections are really excuses. When this happens our call to action is to instill confidence, remove risk, and reassure them that everything will be okay. Or to make it easy to remember, deliver the 3 C's: Confidence, Certainty, and Comfort. But we also know that we may have to do this while we're on the move because in their fearful state, they'll be running and hiding behind every excuse they can find. By definitively solving the problem and *closing*, you are closing that problem. Every time you close a problem, one by one you are closing every door they try to hide behind. Eventually there's no escape. They'll have to face their fear and choose. Choose between staying with all the problems they've complained to you about, or have this great future you are offering them.

Your prospect doesn't have all the funds (but says he'd purchase if he did)? No worries. You'll break the payment up for him, so he won't have any issue. Problem *solved*. But when you ask how he would like to make that first payment, that problem becomes *closed*. Coming up with the funds is no longer an issue. Next, if he's hesitant on making that first payment because he'd like to do some due diligence first, then that's okay too. You'll help him with his research by sending a list of clients that have worked with you personally, and he can ask them about their experience firsthand. If something were to come up in his due diligence that contradicts anything you've said, you'll gladly refund his payment. And you'll even put that in writing, so he can be one hundred percent confident in his decision. Another problem solved! But it's when you ask for the email address he would like this agreement sent to, that closes that problem because that's when the discussion about that issue ends. When overcoming objections, it's not enough to solve the problem, we must close so we put the focus back on the prospect to make a decision. Otherwise the solution you offered to their objection is still open for debate.

When you close after solving every objection, you are forcing them to choose. And every time they choose to say NO out of fear, when they know they should be saying YES, the voice in their head starts getting involved. It's one thing to make a bad decision out of fear. But it's another to continue making bad decision after bad decision. With each bad decision it becomes harder to justify to ourselves. By overcoming multiple objections and closing multiple times, you are putting the prospect in a position to make a series of decisions, not just one. If they make a series of bad decisions, it'll become increasingly harder to hide from their own voice.

> **Side Note:** That last statement is only true if your rebuttal definitively solves the problem. Repeatedly closing without resolving the issue is just annoying and pushes your prospect away. On top of that, if you don't put the issue to bed, it lingers and keeps coming back. And every time they have to repeat themselves about this issue you're not resolving, that problem grows in size. You want to crush a monster when it's

a baby, not when it gets so big it overpowers you. Just giving a response to an objection, without eliminating it completely, will only make that objection resurface because their dilemma still exists. And every time your prospect repeats those words, he's reinforcing his belief that the issue is too great to move forward with you. Take the time to solve the problem for your prospect so that it's truly no longer an issue for them and they no longer need to repeat it.

Tie the Objection to their Pain

The power behind this process is that our prospect's words are what create the impact, not ours. We structure the conversation in a way that gets them to say everything we'd love to tell them. Since it's coming from their mouth, those words mean so much more. Since we're at the final stages of closing the deal and the prospect has reservations, now would be a great time to remind them of what they've said earlier. If we link the pain that they've experienced to the objection they are giving you, then they can see that their objections *are* the very problem. It's that same way of thinking that got them there in the first place. If they want a different result, they must think and act differently.

Every component of this system works together and is strategically designed to get the prospect through the buying journey as fast as possible. In Discovery when you were building leverage on the pain, they were telling you all the pain that came about from their problem. We want to use that to remind them why they should move forward.

Let's look at how this can be done:

Example #1: Earlier Discovery:

You: *Out of curiosity, why is fixing this important to you personally?*

Prospect: *I feel like I'm working so hard and not getting anywhere. I'm burning myself out.*

Example #1: Overcoming Objections:

Prospect: *I can't commit to this right now. The timing isn't right.*

You: *When would be the right time to stop working so hard since you are not getting anywhere? When should you stop burning yourself out?*

Example #2: Earlier Discovery:

You: *How much do you think this problem has cost you in the last 3 years?*

Prospect: *It's cost me a lot more than money, but in just money alone I'd say over $300k.*

Example #2: Overcoming Objections:

Prospect: *I can't afford to make a big investment like this.*

You: *You said that this problem has cost you over $300k in the last few years alone. How can you afford not to fix it? And that's just money. Think about what it's cost you emotionally, in your relationships, etc.*

Chapter 15

Final Thoughts

Justify the Decision with Logic

People buy with emotion and justify with logic. After you get the verbal agreement or the handshake, there's a window between that moment and the moment the contract is signed, or payment is made. That window is when the prospect thinks about the decision they just made and have to justify it both to themselves and to others. If they can't, they simply get buyer's remorse and change their mind. You can make this easy for them by giving them the justification they need. Remind them why this was a great decision, so they have those talking points ready for the conversation they'll inevitably have with themselves or others.

When we want something bad enough, we can pretty much justify anything. So remorse shouldn't be too much of an issue for us because this sales process is designed to create a massive amount of desire. Nevertheless, we want to make our process bulletproof and to strategically account for everything. See, this process isn't just about getting someone emotionally charged to say YES, it's about helping them go from complete stranger to new client in the most efficient, effective, and enjoyable way. We do this by breaking up the buyer's journey into a series of small decisions, while structuring the process to align with each of those decisions in the sequence and the manner they are made.

Although all these new clients will have more than enough ways to justify this decision, we can't create an amazing process and intentionally disregard how the very final decision is made during a purchase. So, for good measure, as our departing gift of this experience, let's make sure that we're completely prepared to remind the prospect why this was a great *logical* decision. With that cherry on top, they now have completed the trifecta. By discovering problems, they felt the pain of why they **have to** make the change. In your presentation they felt the pleasure of what things will be like with your solution in place, which made them **want to** make the change. And by reminding them of the logic of this decision, they have the confirmation that they **should** make the change because it was the right thing to do.

Sales is a Performance: Prepare and Practice

Remember, sales is a performance. So, rehearse! Be an architect that designs the perfect process. Anticipate everything. Write out your discovery questions, your presentation, and your closes. Write down every objection you can think of and practice the 4-Step process to overcome these objections. Practice your delivery: it's more important than what you say.

Repetition

The more times you do this, the better you'll get. Get out there and go for volume at first just so you get accustomed to the process. In the beginning some parts may feel awkward for you (like asking someone how they feel about their problems) but after a few times you'll get completely comfortable. In fact, you'll start to notice these practices all around you. Watch the media interview people who just experienced a hardship. They literally ask those same provoking questions to get the emotion out of the person they're interviewing, and out of us viewers. They say things like, "What was going through your mind when X happened?" or, "How did it make you feel to see Y?" You'll notice that never once does anyone say, "How did I feel? What do you mean how did I feel? I just told you that someone I love got hit by a train!" The reason that never happens is because people simply respond to your questions. Ask questions that arouse feelings and you will take a massive step to closing more sales.

Repetition will make you smoother. It will create confidence in you and that confidence will transfer over to your prospect. Confidence is the opposite of fear. Therefore, the more you repeat this process, the fewer objections your prospects will have and the higher your conversions will be. Set a goal to get 100 presentations out of the way. You won't need 100 to be good - in fact you'll be amazed at what happens by only your fifth. But I want you to be unstoppable. You now have the formula to generate a huge pipeline, so you'll get to one hundred quicker than you think. Assume that's the price of admission to play in the big leagues. Go for it, because everything you want in life is just outside your comfort zone.

Getting Help

The purchase of this book entitles you to one free 30-minute strategy session to brainstorm on how to incorporate the Client Machine methodology in your organization. In this fast-paced session, you and a member of my team will identify the current processes that are broken and give you recommendations, so you can build a fully functioning client machine. To redeem your strategy session, go to: www.client-machine.com/strategysession

Made in the USA
San Bernardino, CA
07 August 2018